*Elizabethan Drama
and the Viewer's Eye*

Elizabethan Drama and the Viewer's Eye

by Alan C. Dessen

The University of North Carolina Press
Chapel Hill

Copyright © *1977 by*
The University of North Carolina Press
All rights reserved
Manufactured in the United States of America
ISBN 0-8078-1291-9
Library of Congress Catalog Card Number 76-26593

Library of Congress Cataloging in Publication Data

Dessen, Alan C   1935 –
  Elizabethan drama and the viewer's eye.

  Bibliography: p.
  Includes index.
    1.   English drama—Early modern and Elizabethan,
1500–1600—History and criticism.   2.   Theater—
England—History.   3.   Shakespeare, William, 1564–
1616—Dramatic production.   I.   Title.
PR651.D4   822'.3'09   76-26593
ISBN 0-8078-1291-9

To Murph and Ashland

Contents

Preface

To present another study of Shakespeare and Elizabethan drama requires an act of faith by the author and an implicit plea for his audience's willing suspension of disbelief. I can only hope that the approach argued for in chapter 1 and pursued in subsequent chapters, an approach that draws upon the insights of the critic, the historian, and the director, may provide arguments and an angle of vision not duplicated elsewhere. My many debts to existing scholarship will appear obvious. Since so many plays are covered in this study, many of them much discussed elsewhere, and since several larger, complex problems are raised, I have chosen to forego extensive acknowledgment of my many debts in the text and notes so as not to drown my argument in a sea of critical and scholarly troubles. Instead, in the bibliography I have called attention to a large number of relevant and stimulating studies.

My special thanks are due to the editors of *Shakespeare Studies* and *English Literary Renaissance* for permission to use materials originally published in those journals; to my students and colleagues at Wisconsin, Northwestern, North Carolina, and the Institute of Renaissance Studies of the Oregon Shakespearean Festival; and to those individuals who showed me that there were more things in theater than were dreamt of in my original philosophy, especially Tim Sloan, Homer Swander, Elizabeth Cole, and Audrey Stanley. For Cynthia, Michael, and Sarah, the rest is silence.

Note on Texts and Old Spelling

All quotations and stage directions from Shakespeare are taken from *The Riverside Shakespeare*, edited by G. Blakemore Evans (Boston, 1974). Elsewhere, I have used modern spelling editions of Elizabethan plays whenever possible, such as those in the Revels Plays series (cited as Revels) and the Regents Renaissance Drama series (cited as RRD). Such editions are noted the first time a play is quoted in any detail and not thereafter. For some of the morality plays, I have used the nineteenth-century Hazlitt's Dodsley and checked the passages and stage directions against facsimile editions.

For a few plays (and for some nondramatic passages in chapter 1) I have used old spelling editions and then modernized the spelling. For example, all quotations from the Tudor Facsimile Texts (cited as TFT) and the Malone Society Reprints (cited as MSR) have been modernized. I take such liberties for two reasons. First, the comparison between Shakespeare and his contemporaries already is invidious enough without having the swan of Avon speak to the modern reader in modern spelling while Jonson, Dekker, and many lesser dramatists struggle along in their archaic terms. Furthermore, since relatively little close textual analysis is offered in this study (and much of that is devoted to Shakespeare), the pitfalls in such modernizing are more than offset by the added ease for some readers.

To avoid inconsistencies in my own text, I have silently made a few other minor changes in quoted passages (such as regularizing the use of italics and Roman type in stage directions).

*Elizabethan Drama
and the Viewer's Eye*

Chapter 1

Elizabethan Drama
and the Modern Reader

For centuries the plays of Shakespeare have functioned as a Rorschach test wherein individuals and even entire cultures consciously or unconsciously have discovered themselves. Nor have such discoveries been jealously guarded as private stock. Rather, the public periodically has been offered proclamations (usually accompanied by the flourish of rhetorical trumpets) of decisively new ways to journey upon this well-traveled road, proclamations that often claim to account not only for Shakespeare but for all of Elizabethan drama. After experiencing a series of such breakthroughs or new looks, the interested reader - or playgoer may be pardoned if he maintains (at the least) a polite skepticism. Without being charged with complacency, that reader—whether historian or critic or director—justifiably can question the need for any "new" approaches. Miranda's "brave new world" can be overshadowed by Prospero's " 'tis new to thee."

But the very existence of such diverse constituencies—the historians, the critics, the directors—suggests a problem that has not been (and may never be) resolved. The exigencies of university teaching have led to a greater and greater "critical" emphasis in treatments of Elizabethan drama, an approach suited to students who brandish "relevance" as their banner and are unwilling or unable to differentiate Shakespeare from Harold

Pinter (or John Barth or Stanley Kubrick). In contrast, the accolades of the scholarly world often are awarded to those who pursue disciplines somewhat distanced from the give and take of undergraduate teaching, such as dramatic history, stage reconstruction, textual study, and the history of ideas. Actors and directors dealing with Shakespeare and his contemporaries work in yet a third sphere, faced as they are with paying audiences who demand entertainment and coherence in terms amenable to the contemporary mood and expectations. To many a director, the critic's subtle insights into motivation or poetic nuances are just as useless as a reconstruction of the Swan Theater or debates over sullied/sallied/solid flesh.

No Moses is at hand to lead historians, critics, and directors to that promised land of harmony and mutual respect, especially since these divergent reactions are a product not merely of the complexities of Elizabethan drama but, more basically, of the much-discussed fragmentation of our contemporary society and sensibility. Many of the combatants in this conflict, moreover, undoubtedly are content with the present state of the battlefield. A director might feel quite lost if deprived of the academic critic or historian as his *bête noire*, while the traditional scholar probably would be equally unhappy if unable to shake his finger at the excesses of current productions. Regardless of the fates of scholars and directors, the Shakespearean critic will continue to practice his craft as long as even one journal remains solvent.

Yet occasionally the critic-teacher's drive to communicate, the scholar-historian's rage for order, and the theatergoer's belief in the importance of live productions combine to produce a study such as this which attempts to speak to all three constituencies. My central thesis is painfully simple. Without disparaging historian, critic, or director, I suggest that all three angles of vision are equally important if we are to gain the fullest possible understanding of drama in the age of Shakespeare. A related (and equally unrevolutionary) thesis is that reading an Elizabethan play should involve more than only attending to the words on a page and that full appreciation and understanding often result from that "more." During recent years, repetition of this latter point may have turned it into yet another critical cliché, but the ramifications of "the play's the thing" have not been explored in depth. The critics who follow this new war cry are just beginning to think like directors and to learn from the historians.

My purpose in this introductory chapter is to justify my project to these three groups. In nonpolemical terms I hope to eliminate some impediments hindering a marriage of true minds.[1]

Let us start with the domain of the historian. From the legacy of information bequeathed to us by the Elizabethans, what if anything can we determine about the theatrical experience in the age of Shakespeare? Did the Elizabethans recognize a distinction between a play on the page and a play on the stage? Were there appeals other than the poetry that drew popular audiences into the theater? What evidence remains about the efficacy of Elizabethan plays in performance before the original audiences?

To the latter question Hamlet provides one possible response. Citing what may have been an Elizabethan cliché, he notes

> *That guilty creatures sitting at a play*
> *Have by the very cunning of the scene*
> *Been strook so to the soul, that presently*
> *They have proclaim'd their malefactions:*

$$[2. 2. 589-92]$$

1. Obviously, I am not the first to make such an attempt. Most recent studies, however, have emphasized heroes and villains (the "trendy" director who is not "true to score") and have not fully developed the potential contribution of the historian. See the first section of my bibliography for a selective yet lengthy list of the voices in this modern stage quarrel.

Before dismissing such a statement as merely the rationalizing of a dilatory Dane thinking too precisely on the event, the modern reader should be reminded that Thomas Heywood, near the end of his *Apology for Actors* (1612), cites two such stories. First he records a performance of a lost play, *The History of Friar Francis,* in which a woman who doted on a young gentleman had "mischievously and secretly murdered her husband, whose ghost haunted her, and at diverse times in her most solitary and private contemplations, in most horrid and fearful shapes, appeared, and stood before her." When this scene was acted, a woman in the audience ("till then of good estimation and report") suddenly cried out: "Oh my husband, my husband! I see the ghost of my husband fiercely threatening and menacing me." When questioned by the people around her, she revealed ("unurged") that seven years earlier she too had murdered her husband to gain such a gentleman, a husband "whose fearful image personated itself in the shape of that ghost"; as Heywood had stated earlier, "her conscience at this presentment" was "extremely troubled." Thanks to the "cunning of the scene," in Hamlet's terms, "the murderess was apprehended, before the justices further examined, and by her voluntary confession after condemned." For the doubters, Heywood adds: "That this is true, as well by the report of the actors as the records of the town, there are many eye-witnesses of this accident yet living, vocally to confirm it." A paragraph later, moreover, Heywood provides an even longer account of a group of English actors in Amsterdam performing a scene in which a man is murdered by a group of laborers who drive a nail into his temples. The reaction of "a woman of great gravity" in the audience (who is "strangely amazed") is then coupled with the discovery, "in the ripping up of a grave," of "a fair skull, with a great nail pierced quite through the brain-pan." According to Heywood, "at the report of this accident, the woman, out of the trouble of her afflicted conscience, discovered a former murder."[2]

The modern reader may remain skeptical about such stories which so neatly serve Heywood's larger purpose—to establish the legitimacy of a medium often under attack for encouraging crime and vice. To the doubter, moreover, Hamlet's formulation, although a necessary part of Shakespeare's dramatic fiction, need not apply to a Claudius in the audience watching *Hamlet*. Nonetheless, such stories and comments do correspond to other passages that also testify to the evocative power of Elizabethan productions. For example, critics today rarely praise the dramatic illusion created by the plays of Beaumont and Fletcher, but Thomas Palmer, in his commendatory verses for the 1647 Folio, writes:

> *How didst thou sway the theatre! make us feel*
> *The players' wounds were true, and their swords, steel!*
> *Nay, stranger yet, how often did I know*
> *When the spectators ran to save the blow?*
> *Frozen with grief we could not stir away*
> *Until the Epilogue told us 'twas a play.*[3]

Even more bizarre is the story told by Edmund Gayton of "a passionate butcher" watching a play who, "seeing Hector overpowered by Myrmidons, got upon the stage, and with his good baton took the true Trojan's part so stoutly, that he routed the Greeks, and railed upon them loudly for a company of cowardly slaves to assault one man with so much odds. He struck moreover such an especial acquaintance with Hector, that for a long time Hector could not obtain leave of him to be killed, that the play might go on; and the cudgelled Myrmidons durst not enter again, till Hector, having prevailed upon his unexpected second,

2. *Apology for Actors*, ed. Richard H. Perkinson, Scholars' Facsimiles and Reprints (New York, 1941), G1 verso–G2 verso. In this and many subsequent quotations (from Palmer, Gayton, Nashe, Webbe, Puttenham, Gosson, Moryson, and Willis) I have modernized the spelling.

3. *Comedies and Tragedies Written by Francis Beaumont and John Fletcher* (London, 1647), F2 verso.

returned him over the stage again into the yard from whence he came."[4] At the least, such an anecdote suggests how deeply an audience could become involved in an Elizabethan performance.

Less graphic but equally suggestive are the comments on the efficacy for the popular audience of the history plays. Thomas Nashe observes in 1592 that the subject of such plays

is borrowed out of our English chronicles wherein our forefathers' valiant acts (that have lain long buried in rusty brass and worm-eaten books) are revived, and they themselves raised from the grave or oblivion, and brought to plead their aged honours in open presence: . . . How would it have joyed brave Talbot (the terror of the French) to think that after he had lain two hundred years in his tomb, he should triumph again on the stage, and have his bones new embalmed with the tears of ten thousand spectators at least (at several times), who, in the tragedian that represents his person, imagine they behold him fresh bleeding.[5]

Similarly, in his *Apology* (B4 recto), Heywood speaks in glowing terms of "our domestic histories," asking, "What English blood seeing the person of any bold English man presented and doth not hug his fame, and hunny at his valor, pursuing him in his enterprise with his best wishes?" What English prince, he continues, watching the victories of Edward III in France, "would not be suddenly inflamed with so royal a spectacle"? For both Nashe and Heywood, the history plays appeal successfully to the hearts (and tear ducts) of the popular audience.

Given such lively accounts of Elizabethan drama in performance, we should not be surprised to discover that even by the early seventeenth century authors could take for granted the distinction between plays on the page and on the stage. Thus, John Marston argues that "comedies are writ to be spoken, not read. Remember the life of these things consists in action."[6] Else-

---

4. *Pleasant Notes upon Don Quixot* (London, 1654), p. 3, cited by Gerald Eades Bentley, *The Jacobean and Caroline Stage* (Oxford, 1967), 5:1345–46.
5. Ronald B. McKerrow, ed., *The Works of Thomas Nashe* (London, 1904), 1:212.
6. *The Fawn*, ed. Gerald A. Smith, RRD (Lincoln, Neb., 1965), p. 5.

where Marston apologizes to the reader of the printed edition "that scenes invented merely to be spoken should be enforcively published to be read"; rather, he hopes "that the unhandsome shape which this trifle in reading presents may be pardoned for the pleasure it once afforded you when it was presented with the soul of lively action."[7] Similarly, George Chapman (whose plays usually are not cited for their stageworthy qualities) states that "scenical representation" provides "personal and exact life" for any history and adds "lustre, spirit, and apprehension."[8] William Webbe calls attention to two kinds of poets, "either such as desire to be liked of on stages, as comedy and tragedy writers, or such as would be registered in libraries." For Webbe, "those on stages have special respect to the motions of the mind, that they may stir both the eyes and ears of their beholders," while the latter variety "take good advisement in their works, that they may satisfy the exact judgments of learned men in their studies."[9]

The most extensive and suggestive discussion of the advantages of "lively action" on stage is provided by Heywood in his *Apology for Actors*. Perhaps echoing Sidney's treatment of history, philosophy, and poetry, he compares oratory, painting, and drama.

7. *The Malcontent*, ed. M. L. Wine, RRD (Lincoln, Neb., 1964), pp. 4–5.

8. Thomas Marc Parrott, ed., *The Plays of George Chapman: The Tragedies* (New York, 1961), 2:341.

9. "A Discourse of English Poetrie," *Elizabethan Critical Essays*, ed. G. Gregory Smith (Oxford, 1904), 1:300. In his dedication to *The Gentleman of Venice*, James Shirley observes that his comedy "had once a singular grace and lustre from the scene, when it enjoyed the life of action" (William Gifford and Alexander Dyce, eds., *The Dramatic Works and Poems of James Shirley* [London, 1833], 5:3). In Thomas Middleton's *A Mad World, My Masters*, Follywit (posing as the leader of an itinerant troupe) tells his uncle that "we could do all to the life of action, sir, both for the credit of your worship's house and the grace of our comedy" (RRD edition, ed. Standish Henning [Lincoln, Neb., 1965], p. 88, 5. 1. 116–17). According to Sir Richard Baker (died 1645), "a play read, hath not half the pleasure of a play acted: for though it have the pleasure of ingenious speeches; yet it wants the pleasure of graceful action: and we may well acknowledge, that gracefulness of action, is the greatest pleasure of a play" (*Theatrum Triumphans*, [London, 1670], p. 34).

A description is only a shadow received by the ear but not perceived by the eye: so lively portraiture is merely a form seen by the eye, but can neither show action, passion, motion, or any other gesture, to move the spirits of the beholder to admiration: but to see a soldier shaped like a soldier, walk, speak, act like a soldier: to see a Hector all besmeared in blood, trampling upon the bulks of kings. A Troilus returning from the field. . . . To see as I have seen, Hercules in his own shape hunting the boar, knocking down the bull, taming the hart, fighting with Hydra. . . . Oh these were sights to make an Alexander . . . so bewitching a thing is lively and well spirited action, that it hath power to new mold the hearts of the spectators and fashion them to the shape of any noble and notable attempt.

[B3 verso–B4 recto]

Marston, Heywood, and others see "lively and well spirited action" as the soul of drama. Both would agree with Hamlet and Webbe that the play's the thing for the eye as well as the ear of the audience, especially if the dramatist's goal is "to new mold the hearts of the spectators"—to catch their consciences.

Unfortunately, Heywood's *Apology* is the only document in the age of Shakespeare written by a knowledgeable figure sympathetic to the popular drama. Without such documents and without detailed accounts of contemporary performances, the historian has difficulty producing solid evidence about Elizabethan productions, not to mention reactions to the staging of specific plays. The modern reader, however, can gain some insights from the diatribes of writers hostile to the drama. Thus George Puttenham, in his disgust with popular audiences, scornfully notes their preference for vivid staging over the subtleties of the verse: "The common people, who rejoice much to be at plays and enterludes, and besides their natural ignorance, have at all such times their ears so attentive to the matter, and their eyes upon the shows of the stage, that they take little heed to the cunning of the rime, and therefore be as well satisfied with that which is gross, as with any other finer and more delicate."[10]

10. *The Arte of English Poesie*, ed. Gladys Doidge Willcock and Alice Walker (Cambridge, 1936), p. 82.

Similarly, when Volumnia, another figure hostile to popular tastes, gives Coriolanus instructions on the gestures needed to win back the support of the plebeians, she observes that "in such business / Action is eloquence, and the eyes of th' ignorant / More learned than the ears" (3. 2. 75–77). Stephen Gosson not only testifies to the visual appeal of the popular drama but also characterizes that appeal as a tool of the Devil: "For the eye, beside the beauty of the houses and the stages, he [the Devil] sendeth in garish apparel, masques vaunting, tumbling, dancing of jigs, galliards, morrisses, hobbyhorses, showing of juggling casts; nothing forgot that might serve to set out the matter with pomp, or ravish the beholders with variety of pleasure." Gosson believes such pomp and stage activity can have a hypnotic effect upon the eye of the beholder, for "being moved with variety of shows, of events, of music, the longer we gaze, the more we crave, yea so forcible they are, that afterwards being but thought upon, they make us seek for the like another time."[11]

Several of the dramatists not sympathetic to popular tastes also comment upon "the eyes of th' ignorant." In his Prologue to *The Doubtful Heir* (1640), a play intended for the Blackfriars but presented at the Globe, James Shirley rules out the visual treats that this audience might expect:

> No shows, no dance, and, what you most delight in,
> Grave understanders, here's no target-fighting
> Upon the stage, all work for cutlers barr'd;
> No bawdry, nor no ballads; this goes hard;
> But language clean; and, what affects you not,
> Without impossibilities the plot:
> No clown, no squibs, no devil in't. [12]

Equally caustic comments are scattered through the works of Ben Jonson. Early in his career, in the prologue to *Cynthia's*

---

11. *Plays Confuted in Five Actions*, reprinted in William Carew Hazlitt, ed., *The English Drama and Stage under the Tudor and Stuart Princes 1543–1664* (London, 1869), pp. 192, 206.
12. Gifford and Dyce, eds., *Dramatic Works*, 4:279.

Revels (1600), Jonson announces that he has found "new ways to come to learned ears" and cites his priorities as "words, above action: matter, above words." Later in his career, when he returned to the public stage after a lapse of ten years, he has the Prologue to *The Staple of News* (1626) instruct the audience:

> For your own sakes, not his, he bade me say,
> Would you were come to hear, not see a play.
> Though we his actors must provide for those,
> Who are our guests, here, in the way of shows,
> The maker hath not so; he'ld have you wise,
> Much rather by your ears, than by your eyes.

The Prologue for the performance at court describes the same play as directed at scholars who "can judge, and fair report / The sense they hear, above the vulgar sort / Of nut-crackers, that only come for sight."[13] The so-called vulgar or ignorant audiences apparently demanded (and, by implication, usually received) elaborate "shows" or stimulation for the eye which, according to Puttenham and Gosson, could overpower or "ravish" them.

The most striking account of the nonverbal appeal of Elizabethan plays is provided by Fynes Moryson, an English traveler on the continent. The English theatrical troupe which Moryson saw in Frankfort had "neither a complete number of actors, nor any good apparel, nor any ornament of the stage, yet the Germans, not understanding a word they said, both men and women, flocked wonderfully to see their gesture and action, rather than hear them, speaking English which they understood not, and pronouncing pieces and patches of English plays, which myself and some English men there present could not hear without great wearisomeness."[14] According to Moryson's ac-

13. C. H. Herford and Percy and Evelyn Simpson, eds., *Ben Jonson*, 11 vols. (Oxford, 1925–1952), 4:43; 6:282–83. I have modernized the spelling in this and subsequent quotations from this edition.

14. Charles Hughes, ed., *Shakespeare's Europe: A Survey of the Condition of Europe at the End of the 16th Century*, 2nd ed. (New York, 1967), p. 304.

count, "gesture and action" could become an end in themselves, transcending not only the poetic medium but the language barrier as well. Or, to borrow from *The Winter's Tale* the reported reaction to the discovery of Perdita's identity, "there was speech in their dumbness, language in their very gesture" (5. 2. 13–14).

Moryson's players may have lacked good apparel and ornaments of the stage, but their counterparts in the Globe and Fortune and Rose and Swan suffered under no such handicap. For example, in 1613, Sir Henry Wotton writes: "The King's players had a new play, called *All is True*, representing some principal pieces of the reign of Henry VIII, which was set forth with many extraordinary circumstances of pomp and majesty, even to the matting of the stage; the Knights of the Order with their Georges and garters, the Guards with their embroidered coats, and the like."[15] Noteworthy opportunities for such displays exist in many Elizabethan plays: processions, weddings, tournaments, masques, state scenes. For special occasions, moreover, the dramatist could call upon special effects. To suggest the pyrotechnics possible on the Elizabethan stage, Andrew Gurr cites Heywood's stage directions in his extravaganza, *The Silver Age* (1611): "*Enter* Pluto *with a club of fire, a burning crown . . . and a guard of Devils, all with burning weapons*"; "*Jupiter appears in his glory under a rainbow*"; "*Thunder, lightnings,* Jupiter *descends in his majesty, his thunderbolt burning. . . . As he toucheth the bed it fires, and all flies up.*"[16] Philip Henslowe's inventory, compiled in 1598, includes a fascinating array of distinctive stage properties, including: two steeples, a chime of bells, and a beacon; a rock; a cage; a tomb; a hellmouth; the city of Rome; the cloth of the sun and the moon; Cerberus's three heads; a tree of

---

15. Wotton to Sir Edmund Bacon, 1613, cited by E. K. Chambers, *William Shakespeare: A Study of Facts and Problems* (Oxford, 1930), 2:344.

16. Gurr, *The Shakespearean Stage 1574–1642* (Cambridge, 1970), p. 122. Throughout this study the dates attached to plays are drawn from Alfred Harbage, *Annals of English Drama 975–1700*, rev. S. Schoenbaum (London, 1964).

golden apples; a great horse with his legs; and a cauldron for the Jew.[17] The cumulative effect of this list, Wotton's letter, and Heywood's stage directions can be misleading, for, as will be noted later, most moments in Elizabethan productions involve only actors and a bare stage. But for major scenes or special occasions, large-scale, even spectacular, effects were possible.

Another way to provide theatrical treats was to bring on stage such bizarre figures as gods, goddesses, ghosts, devils, monsters, and bears. In 1582, Gosson snidely describes contemporary romantic drama as "but the adventures of an amorous knight, passing from country to country for the love of his lady, encountering many a terrible monster made of brown paper."[18] Although members of a play-within-a-play troupe in the late 1590s agreed that such "brown-paper stuff" could no longer gull their audiences,[19] more sophisticated special effects (as in *The Silver Age*) could supersede the earlier devices. Heywood's account of *Friar Francis* cited earlier tells of a "horrid and fearful" ghost, and, if stage directions and internal evidence are to be believed, such eerie presences were a staple part of the dramatic fare. In his *Black Book*, Thomas Middleton describes a figure as having "a head of hair like one of my devils in *Doctor Faustus*, when the old theatre cracked and frighted the audience."[20] Similarly, John Melton cites a production of the same play in 1620 in which "a man may behold shag-haired devils run roaring over the stage with squibs in their mouths, while drummers make thunder in the tiring-house, and the twelve-penny hirelings make artificial lightning in their heavens."[21] Indeed,

17. R. A. Foakes and R. T. Rickert, eds., *Henslowe's Diary* (Cambridge, 1961), pp. 319–21.

18. *Plays Confuted in Five Actions*, p. 181.

19. Sir Oliver Owlet's players in *Histriomastix*. See H. Harvey Wood, ed., *The Plays of John Marston* (London, 1939), 3:283.

20. A. H. Bullen, ed., *The Works of Thomas Middleton* (London, 1886), 8:13.

21. *Astrologaster* (London, 1620), p. 31, cited by John D. Jump in his introduction to the Revels edition of *Doctor Faustus* (London, 1962), p. lix. All subsequent quotations from *Doctor Faustus* are from this edition.

the story of the provincial performance of *Doctor Faustus* in which the players discovered an extra devil in their midst provides eloquent testimony to the theatrical vitality behind such presentation.[22]

Again, the modern reader often can sense the theatricality only partially obscured by hostile comments. Shirley, in the Prologue cited earlier, comments scornfully upon what the popular audience might expect: shows, dances, target-fighting, "work for cutlers," bawdry, ballads, clowns, squibs, and devils. Far better known is Jonson's critique of "th'ill customs of the age" in his Prologue to the revised *Every Man In His Humour*. Typically, Jonson refuses to give the audience what they want; he will not "with three rusty swords, / And help of some few foot and half-foot words, / Fight over York and Lancaster's long jars, / And in the tiring-house bring wounds to scars." Rather, he is offering a play "as other plays should be":

> *Where neither Chorus wafts you o'er the seas,*
> *Nor creaking throne comes down, the boys to please,*
> *Nor nimble squib is seen, to make afear'd*
> *The gentlewomen, nor roll'd bullet heard*
> *To say, it thunders, nor tempestuous drum*
> *Rumbles, to tell you when the storm doth come;*[23]

The "ill customs of the age" that offended Jonson (and, later, Shirley) thereby included swordplay, fireworks, sound effects, and spectacular devices (the creaking throne), all of which could appear a positive side of the Elizabethan theater to a less jaundiced eye.

Another lively critique of the conventions of the popular drama can be found in the Induction to *A Warning for Fair Women* (1599) where Comedy mocks the appeal of Tragedy:

22. See E. K. Chambers, *The Elizabethan Stage* (Oxford, 1923), 3:424, and Jump's introduction, p. lx. The story was probably a fabrication used as propaganda against plays and players.
23. Text used is the RRD edition, ed. J. W. Lever (Lincoln, Neb., 1971), p. 5.

> How some damn'd tyrant, to obtain a crown,
> Stabs, hangs, impoisons, smothers, cutteth throats;
> And then a Chorus too comes howling in,
> And tells us of the worrying of a cat;
> Then of a filthy whining ghost,
> Lapt in some foul sheet, or a leather pilch,
> Comes screaming like a pig half stick'd,
> And cries Vindicta, revenge, revenge:
> With that a little rosin flasheth forth,
> Like smoke out of a tobacco pipe, or a boy's squib:
> Then comes in two or three like to drovers,
> With tailor's bodkins, stabbing one another.
> Is not this trim? is not here goodly things
> That you should be so much accounted of? [24]

Like the Prologues of Jonson and Shirley, Comedy singles out sword (or bodkin) play and also provides some suggestive comments about the staging of ghost scenes. Here, moreover, is a sardonic description of the kind of stage business called for in plays like *The Spanish Tragedy*, *The Tragedy of Hoffman*, and *Antonio's Revenge*, not to mention *Hamlet* and *Macbeth*.

By this point the modern reader may be wondering about the negative or fragmentary evidence so far adduced. Are there no more detailed contemporary accounts than the few sentences cited on *Doctor Faustus* and *Henry VIII*? Simon Forman, for one, recorded his impressions of at least five plays (*Macbeth*, *Cymbeline*, *The Winter's Tale*, *Cox of Collumpton*, and a lost *Richard II*), but his plot summaries provide few details not in the extant texts. [25] Other accounts (such as Gosson on *The Three Ladies of*

24. Text used is the TFT edition, ed. John S. Farmer (1912).
25. For the account of *Cox of Collumpton* see Samuel A. Tannenbaum, *Shaksperian Scraps and Other Elizabethan Fragments* (New York, 1933), p. 14. For Forman's descriptions of the other four plays see E. K. Chambers, *William Shakespeare* (New York, 1930), 2:337–41. Even less informative are the diary and account book of Sir Humphrey Mildmay who, between 1632 and 1643, saw fifty-seven plays and four court masques. Outside of calling some plays "foolish"

London or *The Play of Plays and Pastimes*) are equally uninformative about staging. A comment in Edward Sharpham's *The Fleir*
(1607) suggests that at the end of *A Midsummer Night's Dream*,
Thisbe comically stabbed herself not with the sword but with
the scabbard, but, if the allusion to Shakespeare is accepted, it
remains "the only recorded certain reference to contemporary
stage business in any of Shakespeare's plays."[26] The Peacham
drawing of a moment from the opening scene of *Titus Andronicus*
(see Conclusion) may or may not be a rendition of the actual
staging.[27] Thus, when we start to look for concrete evidence
about theatrical presentation of specific Elizabethan plays, we
quickly move into the realm of conjecture and surmise.

One major exception is R. Willis's record in 1639 of his
memories of a performance of a morality play seen in his boyhood in the 1560s or 1570s:

The play was called *The Cradle of Security*, wherein was personated a king
or some great prince with his courtiers of several kinds, amongst which
three ladies were in special grace with him; and they keeping him in
delights and pleasures, drew him from his graver counsellors, hearing
of sermons, and listening to good counsel, and admonitions, that in the
end they got him to lie down in a cradle upon the stage, where these

and praising Shirley's *The Lady of Pleasure* as "that rare play," he gives no details.
See Bentley, *Jacobean and Caroline Stage*, 2:673–81.
26. William A. Ringler, Jr., "The Number of Actors in Shakespeare's Early
Plays," *The Seventeenth-Century Stage*, ed. Gerald Eades Bentley (Chicago, 1968),
p. 111. For the passage see Sir Edmund Chambers, ed., *The Shakspere Allusion-
Book: A Collection of Allusions to Shakspere from 1591 to 1700* (London, 1932), 1:174.
Another possible allusion has Hamlet perhaps stroking Yorick's skull (*Shakspere
Allusion-Book*, 1:160–61). In Anthony Scoloker's *Daiphantus* (1604), a figure "puts
off his clothes; his shirt he only wears, / Much like mad Hamlet" (*Shakspere
Allusion-Book*, 1:133). The staging of the banquet scene of *Macbeth* may be
reflected in *The Knight of the Burning Pestle* when Jasper, posing as a ghost,
threatens to "come in midst of all thy pride and mirth, / Invisible to all men but
thyself, / And whisper such a sad tale in thine ear / Shall make thee let the cup
fall from thy hand" (act 5, lines 24–27). See the RRD text, ed. John Doebler
(Lincoln, Neb., 1967), p. 95.
27. See E. K. Chambers, "The First Illustration to 'Shakespeare'," *The
Library*, 4th series, 5 (1925): 326–30.

three ladies joining in a sweet song rocked him asleep, that he snorted again, and in the mean time closely conveyed under the cloths where withal he was covered, a vizard like a swine's snout upon his face, with three wire chains fastened thereunto, the other end whereof being holden severally by those three ladies, who fall to singing again, and then discovered his face, that the spectators might see how they had transformed him, going on with their singing. Whilst all this was acting, there came forth of another door at the farthest end of the stage, two old men, the one in blue with a sergeant at arms, his mace on his soldier, the other in red with a drawn sword in his hand, and leaning with the other hand upon the other's shoulder, and so they two went along in a soft pace round about by the skirt of the stage, till at last they came to the cradle, when all the court was in greatest jollity, and then the foremost old man with his mace struck a fearful blow upon the cradle; whereat all the courtiers with the three ladies and the vizard all vanished; and the desolate prince starting up bare faced, and finding himself thus sent for to judgment, made a lamentable complaint of his miserable case, and so was carried away by wicked spirits. This prince did personate in the morall, the wicked of the world; the three ladies, Pride, Covetousness, and Luxury, the two old men, the end of the world, and the last judgment.[28]

From this account a modern reader can sense the flavor of a performance of a play now lost, a play that would scarcely be known if it had survived and, if known, would be ignored or scorned as are most of the late moralities. Yet there can be no question about the efficacy of the performance for at least one viewer, because Willis (some sixty or seventy years later) concludes: "This sight took such impression in me, that when I came towards man's estate, it was as fresh in my memory, as if I had seen it newly acted."

Willis's account, along with the other historical evidence cited in the previous pages, can suggest the potent effect upon the original viewers of Elizabethan performances. But if the historian is temporarily pacified, the critic may in turn ask what

28. *Mount Tabor, or Private Exercises of a Penitent Sinner* (London, 1639), pp. 111–13.

the presence of such a visual or theatrical dimension means for him. Does an awareness of potential effects make any difference in the critic's approach to character or theme or imagery or structure? If Puttenham and Gosson are to be believed, the rich "variety of shows" could so "ravish the beholders with variety of pleasure" that the nuances (such as "the cunning of the rime") could be overshadowed. By emphasizing the visual or theatrical elements of such plays, is the historian or director helping or hindering a critical investigation? Were the Elizabethan dramatists able to harness this potential in their theater or did they lose control (as the stage directions from *The Silver Age* might suggest)?

To consider such questions is the goal of this study. Here, at the outset, let me suggest the value to the critic of an approach that takes into account the viewer's eye. To do so, I propose to examine briefly three quite different plays.

First, consider *Gorboduc*[29] (1562), a static, declamatory tragedy directed at an elite audience and rarely cited for its theatrical virtues. *"The Order and Signification of the Dumb Show Before the Second Act"* reads as follows:

First, the music of cornets began to play, during which came in upon the stage a king accompanied with a number of his nobility and gentlemen. And after he had placed himself in a chair of estate prepared for him, there came and kneeled before him a grave and aged gentleman and offered up a cup unto him of wine in a glass, which the king refused. After him comes a brave and lusty young gentleman and presents the king with a cup of gold filled with poison, which the king accepted, and drinking the same, immediately fell down dead upon the stage, and so was carried thence away by his lords and gentlemen, and then the music ceased. Hereby was signified, that as glass by nature holdeth no poison, but is clear and may easily be seen through, ne boweth by any art; so a faithful counselor holdeth no treason, but is plain and open, ne yieldeth to any undiscreet affection, but giveth wholesome counsel, which the ill-advised prince refuseth. The delight-

29. Text used is the RRD edition, ed. Irby B. Cauthen, Jr. (Lincoln, Neb., 1970).

ful gold filled with poison betokeneth flattery, which under fair seeming of pleasant words beareth deadly poison, which destroyed the
prince that receiveth it. As befell in the two brethren, Ferrex and Porrex, who, refusing the wholesome advice of grave counselors, credited
these young parasites and brought to themselves death and destruction
thereby.

No difficulty exists here for the critic, for even a casual reader
cannot miss the elaborate description of the dumb show and the
careful moralization. But what would have been the theatrical
experience of a member of the original audience not privy to the
printed text? Admittedly, the Chorus at the end of act 2 does
briefly explicate the dumb show:

> Foul fall the traitor false that undermines
> > The love of brethren to destroy them both.
> Woe to the prince that pliant ear inclines
> > And yields his mind to poisonous tale that floweth
> From flattering mouth! And woe to wretched land
> That wastes itself with civil sword in hand!
> > Lo, thus it is, poison in gold to take
> And wholesome drink in homely cup forsake.
>
> [2. 2. 101–8]

The viewer (as opposed to the reader) must wait over three
hundred lines for this explanation (and even then may miss the
full resonance of the gold versus glass cups); nevertheless, the
viewer has a distinct advantage over the reader of the printed
text. Thus, between the dumb show (involving a king, "a grave
and aged gentleman," and "a brave and lusty young gentleman") and the choric explanation he sees two scenes that exhibit
princes (Ferrex, Porrex) who reject their wise counselors (Dor-
dan, Philander) in favor of their parasites (Hermon, Tyndar).
The stage picture presented by the dumb show (king, old adviser, young adviser) is echoed clearly in act 2, scenes 1 and 2; to
heighten the connection, the princes could be wearing crowns
while the costumes or stage properties of their companions

could be reminiscent of the earlier moment. All three moments could be blocked similarly if not identically to emphasize the links. Thus, even though a member of the audience would lack the clear "signification" which the dramatists provide for the reader, he could gain from a performance a total emblematic effect (dumb show, two dramatic examples, moralization) not readily apparent on the printed page. Although the overall thesis may be the same, the effect in performance of even this declamatory play can be significantly different from that evoked by the page.

From the stately *Gorboduc* let us turn to George Wapull's *The Tide Tarrieth No Man*[30] (1576), a representative late morality play with a Vice (Courage), various "estates" figures, banal verse, and an emphatic attack upon materialism. Although a quick reading may reveal little structural coherence to the critic, the play when staged could have considerable dramatic integrity. For example, the title page offers us a list whereby the eighteen parts can be handled by only four actors; the actor who is to play the demanding role of the Vice is called upon to double only once. That one instance, however, is quite suggestive—in the middle of the play the actor playing the Vice must exit only to appear moments later as the poor but honest Debtor who refuses to bribe the Sergeant and therefore is led off to prison (while wealthier figures like No Good Neighborhood and Greediness are able to bend the law). Although this brief scene has an obvious point to make about the corrupt world depicted by the play, it may seem gratuitous to a modern reader concerned with dramatic economy. But the larger purpose of the scene can be grasped only when one takes into account the final moments of the morality. When Courage tries to flee from Faithful Few and Authority (who carries a sword and is addressed in judicial terms), Correction enters and is told "thine office do, / Take here

30. Ed. Ernst Ruhl, *Shakespeare Jahrbuch* 43 (1907): 1–52. I have modernized the spelling.

this caitiff unto the jail" (1813–14). Remember Willis's description of *The Cradle of Security* that concluded with the appearance of two old men, "the one in blue with a sergeant at arms, his mace on his shoulder, the other in red with a drawn sword in his hand"—figures identified as "the end of the world, and the last judgment." Wapull's Authority clearly corresponds to Willis's figure in red bearing a sword, while Correction, whose job is to take offenders to jail, undoubtedly would be costumed as a sergeant or beadle. In the terms of Wapull's play, Correction is a heavenly version of that corrupt sergeant who led off the impoverished debtor (a figure played by the same actor now portraying the Vice). Certainly the blocking for the two figures (arrester and prisoner) could be analogous, whether the second sergeant figure is a carbon copy of the first (taking into account the limited costumes available to a touring troupe) or a sergeant at arms with a mace and dignity in contrast to the corrupt earthly sergeant. The exact stage image (or version of sergeantry) is less important than the larger analogue, however it is implemented, for the two episodes, which could easily be linked visually and theatrically, represent two stages in a process that structures the entire play—the movement from the domination of the Vice and his worldly interpretation of the proverbial title (*carpe diem*) to the emergence of Faithful Few and Christianity with their heavenly version of that same proverb (see lines 43–49). Such links between disparate parts of the play do not turn *The Tide Tarrieth No Man* into great dramatic art, but, as in *Gorboduc*, we can recognize how the experience offered to the viewer's eye in a performance could involve more unity and consistency than would have appeared from a casual reading of the text.

Shakespeare's *The Tempest* lies many dramatic miles from *Gorboduc* and *The Tide Tarrieth No Man*. Certainly recourse to extraverbal effects is not needed to "rescue" this tightly constructed play from charges of formlessness or diffuseness. Critics, in fact, are fond of pointing to the various ways in which disparate actions here form a unified whole. But if attention is paid to the resources of the theater, some of the subtle relationships discovered by the critics can become far more obvious, even for an audience unaccustomed to such analogous actions. For example, there needs no ghost come from the grave to tell us that Caliban's plot against Prospero relates in some way to Antonio's plot against Alonso. But this relationship need not be a critic's arcane discovery unearthed after many close readings. Thus at the end of act 4 the three comic figures appropriate the glistering apparel on the "line" and for their pains are literally hounded off the stage. Their reappearance *"in their stol'n apparel"* (5. 1. 255 s.d.) could have a telling effect if that apparel, even in its bemired state, corresponds to garments worn by figures already on stage. Earlier the audience had been informed that Gonzalo had provided the banished Prospero and his infant daughter with "rich garments, linens, stuffs, and necessaries" (1. 2. 164); the luggage on the line (and now on the backs of the comic threesome) could correspond to the garb of Milan or Naples. More specifically, Caliban could be clothed like Antonio, Stephano like Alonso, and Trinculo like Sebastian. Caliban, moreover, could be the third figure on stage attired as Duke of Milan. In preparation for the denouement, Prospero had put aside his magical robes, sent for his hat and rapier, and had Ariel attire him so the erstwhile magician could appear "as I was sometime Milan" (5. 1. 86).

Given the presence on stage of two figures in similar costumes, consider the telling effect upon the viewer if Caliban appears wearing inappropriate, stolen garments visually analogous to the ducal robes of Milan. Most important, the kinship between Caliban and Antonio (and perhaps Prospero also) no longer would be an abstract relationship suited only to the page but would be a visible, emphatic connection on stage. To a lesser degree, a similar relationship could be heightened through the costuming of Stephano and Trinculo who, in their drunkenness and choice of trash, have functioned as a debased version of the courtiers. To establish the point firmly, a director could supply an instant of self-recognition when Alonso, Antonio, and Sebastian for a moment see the degraded yet perhaps accurate image of what they have been or will continue to be. So when Prospero directs the nobles to "mark but the badges of these men, my lords, / Then say if they be true" (5. 1. 267–68), a similarity in costume between the low comic figures and their supposed betters would add considerable force to the lesson provided for the courtiers and for the audience.

The historian may object that there is no evidence that act 5 of *The Tempest* was staged in this manner under Shakespeare's watchful eye, but the advantage of this stage effect is that it adds nothing new but rather makes apparent to the eye of the viewer a relationship that otherwise would exist only abstractly. Coming at the climax of the play when various threads are being woven together, such a visual identification of Caliban, Antonio, and Prospero could provide a strong sense of unity in diversity —exactly the effect claimed on the basis of other kinds of analysis. As with *Gorboduc* and *The Tide Tarrieth No Man*, the experience of the audience in the theater could be both richer and more coherent than that afforded the reader of the printed page.

If a suspension of disbelief can be elicited from the historian and the critic, what then of the director, certainly the figure most suspicious of another scholarly or critical investigation of Elizabethan drama. No one actively engaged in a performance of a Shakespearean play need be reminded of the distinction between page and stage. In recent years, moreover, critics and scholars with considerable theatrical experience have been among the most active proponents of the "play on stage" point of view. Thus, in a provocative essay, John Russell Brown has taken to task any critic who pays lip service to "understanding the controlling importance of stage performance" but in practice uses "particular theatrical references, none too precisely, as a kind of exfoliation of his discourse on the play." Indeed, Brown sees the critical act as a distortion of the nature of drama, for attempts to "fix" plays—to "establish an inescapable revaluation"—represent a "wholly unwarranted simplification" of a medium which, in production, cannot be held still for examination. Brown's conclusion, which he admits to be extreme, is that direct involvement, "at firsthand, with the process of a play in rehearsal and performance is an inevitable step that must be taken by the responsible critic of Shakespeare's plays."[31]

The strictures and arguments of Brown and others like him, figures with credentials as critics, scholars, and directors, should carry a good deal of weight. Attempts to arrive at a definitive explication of the meaning of any complex play inevitably will be self-defeating, especially when the critic does not take into account the many variables involved in a production. Since critics and scholars often write for each other, the director outside the academic community has every reason to look with suspicion at yet another study that purports to teach him his craft written by someone not in the theater. Although theatrical insights often have flowed into criticism and scholarship, the traffic in the other direction has been much lighter.

Obviously, within a few pages I cannot convince a director or actor of the utility of this study for his purposes. But let us at least make a start with an interesting analogy. About three decades ago, a major figure in the theater, Robert Edmund Jones, offered the following evaluation of American drama in the 1930s.

It is a truism of theatrical history that stage pictures become important only in periods of low dramatic vitality. Great dramas do not need to be illustrated or explained or embroidered. They need only to be brought to life on the stage. The reason we have had realistic stage "sets" for so long is that few of the dramas of our time have been vital enough to be able to dispense with them. That is the plain truth. Actually the best

31. "The Theatrical Element of Shakespeare Criticism," *Reinterpretations of Elizabethan Drama*, ed. Norman Rabkin (New York, 1969), pp. 178, 182–84, 188.

thing that could happen to our theatre at this moment would be for playwrights and actors and directors to be handed a bare stage on which no scenery could be placed, and then told that they must write and act and direct for this stage. In no time we should have the most exciting theatre in the world.[32]

Today we can recognize the truth in Jones's critique and appreciate some of the exciting events he prophesied. But there is a revealing irony in his account. Here, in an age of stage pictures and realistic sets, a highly knowledgeable figure (whose credits include the designing of several major productions of Shakespeare's plays) cites the bare stage as an innovation, a step forward, a fruitful break with present practice. Though not specifically, Jones is arguing (consciously or unwittingly) for the advantages of Elizabethan over contemporary staging, since dramatists in the age of Shakespeare *did* have such a stage and *did* produce exciting theater. My purpose is not to belittle Jones (who may have had the Elizabethans in mind), but rather to note how modern dramatists and directors could be so immersed in the details of the present that they could lose sight of an instructive lesson from the past. A model was there, but few were looking.

Although it is relatively easy through hindsight to see both the assets and the liabilities in Jones's critique, to categorize what is "right" and "wrong" in our own theater is far more difficult. The most influential voice of recent years has been that of Antonin Artaud who argued for "no more masterpieces" and urged instead a theater of cruelty "in which violent physical images crush and hypnotize the sensibility of the spectator seized by the theater as by a whirlwind of higher forces."[33] Peter Brook has commented upon Artaud's concept of a Holy Theater—"a theatre working like the plague, by intoxication, by infection, by analogy, by magic; a theatre in which the play, the

---

32. *The Dramatic Imagination* (New York, 1941), pp. 134–35.
33. *The Theater and Its Double*, trans. Mary Caroline Richards (New York, 1958), pp. 74–83.

event itself, stands in place of a text." Brook asks: "Is there another language, just as exacting for the author, as a language of words? Is there a language of actions, a language of sounds— a language of word-as-part-of movement, of word-as-lie, word-as-parody, of word-as-rubbish, of word-as-contradiction, of word-shock or word-cry? If we talk of the more-than-literal, if poetry means that which crams more and penetrates deeper—is this where it lies?" Brook's call for "another language" is linked to his sense of what is missing on the contemporary stage. He observes that "our ever-changing language has rarely been richer, and yet it does not seem that the word is the same tool for dramatists that it once was." Today, he argues, "writers seem unable to make ideas and images collide through words with Elizabethan force."[34] One of the most successful modern directors of Shakespeare's plays is offering his critique of modern drama and using Elizabethan drama as one of his yardsticks.

But remember the critique (and the irony) supplied by Jones. If another sense of theater was available in Shakespeare's age but was not seen by the dramatists of the 1930s, is it not possible that "another language," especially "a language of actions," may also be there in Elizabethan plays although largely unnoticed by later critics and directors? In a passage cited earlier, Fynes Moryson called attention to the Elizabethan actors in Germany who somehow transcended the language barrier through their gestures and actions. If we have only recently discovered (or rediscovered) the open stage, it may now be time to discover (or rediscover) the techniques and visual language that go with that open stage. The director who draws upon the skills of the historian and the critic may be able to find "another language" long lost but still recoverable, a language that could add coherence and meaning to both Elizabethan and later plays.

Such possibilities may seem grandiose, especially following the rather modest claims based upon hypothetical stagings of

34. *The Empty Space* (New York, 1968), pp. 48–49.

parts of *Gorboduc*, *The Tide Tarrieth No Man*, and *The Tempest*. But consider the added effect of dramatic emblems or visual analogues when acted out on a bare stage (or hall or innyard)—with no scenery, with minimal use of props and accessories, with no attempt to sustain any illusion of reality. As opposed to the extravagances of the nineteenth century or the endless possibilities of the cinema, such an uncluttered stage not only can free the audience's attention for nuances of poetry but also can free the eye from distraction so that it can focus upon the actors— their postures, their groupings, their costumes, and their part in a patterned movement which is the entire play. In short, here is a stage that can heighten both verbal and visual language. Here, moreover, is a stage upon which was played a body of drama unequaled in our language with a dramaturgy that has yet to be defined adequately and is not irrelevant to the theater of today.

How then are we to define the dramaturgy or sense of theater that lies behind the plays we so much admire? Can we even assume that one set of techniques or one idea of a theater can encompass the complex and diverse dramatic corpus of Elizabethan drama? For example, Joseph W. Donohue, Jr., has recently pointed to the importance for several centuries of English drama of "the affective drama of situation"—an approach first associated with the plays of John Fletcher who, at the end of Shakespeare's career, became the most prominent playwright in London. In this kind of play, according to Donohue, "the intelligible unit is not the thematic part, placed within a coherent series of other parts, but, as in Fletcherian drama, the scene, which exists in effect for its own sake." Such plays, whether Jacobean or Augustan or Romantic, "have a structure based on a series of circumstances and events unconnected by a strict logic of causality (or Aristotelian 'action'); their situations are deliberately brought out of the blue for the purpose of displaying human reactions to extreme and unexpected occurrences."[35]

35. *Dramatic Character in the English Romantic Age* (Princeton, 1970), p. 28.

In contrast to the plays of Fletcher and his successors, however, much of the preceding Elizabethan drama appears to be linked to a sense of "multiple unity" (a term advanced by Madeleine Doran and borrowed from art historians) in which many parts, rarely from only one story line, add up to a larger effect which draws upon a pleasure in "abundant variousness."[36] Extreme versions of such multiplicity of action (like Jonson's *Bartholomew Fair*) become almost unintelligible on the modern stage, while, for pragmatic reasons, modern directors often will pare down the Elizabethan richness to fit a later sense of dramatic focus (the larger group of avenging sons—Fortinbras, Laertes, Pyrrhus—thus must give way to the story of Hamlet). Yet if we keep in mind the uncluttered stage and its potential for establishing visual relationships, we may find (as in my examples from *The Tide Tarrieth No Man* and *The Tempest*) interesting possibilities for a language of action or costume or gesture that could bring alive in the theater the linkages inherent in the concept of "multiple unity." To cite a familiar example, if we note that Brabantio in act 1 (with his mind poisoned by Iago) and Cassio in act 2 (with his degradation occasioned by giving in to his particular weakness) are acting out versions of Othello's tragic pattern, we may be able to stage the initial movement of the continuum that is *Othello* so that it visibly prefigures and illuminates the major sequence of the tragedy, even for an audience unaccustomed to such analogues.

The modern director can learn from the scholar or critic a different, perhaps a neo-Elizabethan, habit of mind, a way of seeing the personae and events of a Shakespearean play not only as an exposition of character but also as an unfolding of a larger pattern that can be enhanced and driven home by action, staging, and gesture. In such a pattern, units or sequences of plays have their own intrinsic interest yet can echo or prefigure each other, thereby yielding a complex multiple unity not ap-

36. *Endeavors of Art* (Madison, 1954), p. 6 and *passim*.

parent to the casual reader or to many an actor or director bound by his own sense of theater. Conversely, the excitement that a director gains by reshaping, cutting, or expanding an Elizabethan play may be at the expense of another kind of excitement present in the original that grows out of divergent parts coalescing into a larger whole before the eyes of the audience. By adding what he takes to be a comprehensible language for his viewers, that director may then be burying the original language which the playwright had incorporated into his own play.

At least part of the problem for directors and for many modern readers results from the complacent notions about "progress" that lurk (often unconsciously) beneath our attitudes toward the drama and culture of the past. It is difficult for anyone, including the historian, *not* to conceive of *The Tide Tarrieth No Man* and *The Cradle of Security* (regardless of its lasting effect upon Willis) as "primitive," and such an evaluation often spills over into our attitude toward such accomplished dramatists as Marlowe, Webster, and even Shakespeare. But we should remember that such plays apparently satisfied a diverse and demanding paying audience of the sort no longer drawn into the theater. Moreover, as Raymond Williams points out in his survey of modern drama, "the history of art is not one of continual evolution into higher and better forms; there is debasement as well as refinement, and a novelty, even a transformation, may be bad as well as good. It would be absurd to imagine that our own contemporary segment from the great arc of dramatic possibility is, because the latest, necessarily the best."[37] Granted, there is no guarantee that attention to the distinctive nature of drama in the age of Shakespeare will yield results fruitful for the modern director. Yet we seem to be going through a lively period in the history of drama in which interesting steps forward or breakthroughs turn out to be (unwitting) rediscoveries of techniques taken for granted by Elizabethan audiences (the open stage, the mixing of actors and

37. *Drama from Ibsen to Brecht* (London, 1968), p. 16.

viewers, extempore improvisations based upon suggestions from the audience[38]). The historian might prove an unforeseen ally for the innovative director.

Let me admit in advance the vulnerability of many of the arguments or analyses that follow. When confronted with some of my suggested stagings or patterns, the historian justly will point to the paucity of evidence; as noted earlier, external evidence about Elizabethan plays in performance is sadly lacking, while reliable stage directions are few and usually are uninformative (*"Dies," "Exit"*). The director, on the other hand, may find that my comments and suggestions, especially when concerned with patterns and themes, are too general and therefore of little practical use. The critic looking for new and exciting interpretations of Elizabethan plays may be disappointed because often I reaffirm in different terms what have become standard readings of major plays. Again, my purpose is not to challenge the findings of the critical literature, but rather to demonstrate how the insights of many astute critics could have been realized in performance before an audience lacking the facilities of the reader in his study. In general, the questions raised here are more important than the answers supplied, for I will have achieved my goal if my reader emerges with a new or even an adjusted angle of vision on this impressive body of dramatic literature. Even partial acceptance of my arguments could establish the important fact that the historian, the critic, and the director stand on common ground when they confront Elizabethan drama.

38. For interaction between players and audience one can turn to almost any Vice in the late moralities (such as Courage in *The Tide Tarrieth No Man*). For improvisations, we are told of Richard Tarlton (the first Elizabethan "star" actor) that "while the queen's players lay in Worcester city to get money, it was his custom for to sing extempore of themes given him"; elsewhere, we hear of "a play in the country, where, as Tarlton's use was, the play being done, every one so pleased to throw up his theme." See Charles Read Baskervill, *The Elizabethan Jig and Related Song Drama* (Chicago, 1929), pp. 99–100.

Chapter 2

Staging and Structure in the Late Morality Play

My point of departure may surprise the critic and the director. Given the distinctive achievement of the drama in the age of Shakespeare, need we be concerned with antecedents? Or, if earlier dramatists and plays are to be considered, why not start with Plautus, Terence, and Seneca or with the Corpus Christi plays or with moralities like *The Castle of Perseverance, Mankind*, and *Everyman*? Why turn to obscure plays like *The Tide Tarrieth No Man* and equally obscure dramatists like Wapull, Fulwell, Lupton, and Wager? Without question, the late moralities lack the sophistication of Roman drama or the intensity of *Everyman* or the broad appeal of the Wakefield cycle. Is this topic merely a sop to the historian and of little interest to the critic or director?

Such questions are valid, and the answers are basic to this study. If we are to make a serious attempt to investigate the relationship between Elizabethan plays and the viewer's eye, we must try, particularly at the outset, to see drama through the eyes of its original viewers rather than our own. Admittedly, we cannot hope to become at one with the original audience of *Hamlet* nor should we establish such retrogression as an ideal. But as Bernard Beckerman aptly observes:

Each time a reader takes up a copy of a play, he also puts on a pair of spectacles. The frame of those spectacles is not plastic or horn but history. The lenses are not optical glass but accumulated dramatic practice and theory. Fashioned by generations of creative and critical theater artists, these glasses are compacted of preconceptions about what constitutes drama and how it produces its effects. Each scene and each act is filtered through these invisible panes before reaching the imagination. . . . Reading an "unfinished" play script depends upon the governing vision of one's spectacles.[1]

A modern reader, for example, may look at *King Lear* through spectacles compacted of notions drawn from Samuel Beckett (or from A. C. Bradley or Sigmund Freud). There is an even subtler danger, moreover, in fashioning our glasses for Elizabethan drama from our reading of Shakespeare alone, a dramatist whose artistry often metamorphoses stock conventions into something rich and strange.

Where then is the stuff that such spectacles are made of? Certainly, the plays of Plautus, Terence, and Seneca can indicate the themes, stock characters, and sense of form inherited by the age of Shakespeare, but the Elizabethans apparently knew (or cared) little about how these plays had been staged and undoubtedly saw them through their own spectacles (as indicated by a play like *The Comedy of Errors*). The craft cycles bequeathed some memorable dramatis personae (like Herod and Mrs. Noah), while no one can question the importance of the morality play's *Humanum Genus* hero for such later protagonists as Doctor Faustus, Othello, and Macbeth. But we should remember that the first permanent public theaters were established outside of London in 1576. During the next decade, while the players and dramatists were discovering the potential in the new facilities and enlarged personnel, there is little evidence of the presence or influence of either the craft cycles or the full-scale moralities as found around 1500. On the other hand, for several decades a lively, professional drama with its own know-how and expertise had been performing moralities (quite different from *Everyman*) and "hybrid" plays (like *Cambises*) all over England. Although

1. *Dynamics of Drama* (New York, 1970), p. 3.

such plays may be unknown and unread today, they represent the fare offered by the popular professional troupes during the formative years of the public theater. If Shakespeare or Marlowe had seen a play in his boyhood, it probably would have been acted in King Cambises's vein (or Courage's) rather than resembling *Everyman* or the Wakefield cycle.

The reader of *Hamlet* may not feel obligated to master all the "hybrid" tragedies written for touring troupes, nor need the reader of *Volpone* turn first to *All for Money* and *Enough is as Good as a Feast*. But if we are to adjust our reading glasses to take into account staging and visual effects, there is no better point of departure than the popular troupe plays of the 1560s and the 1570s, written and presumably performed during the first half of Queen Elizabeth's reign and perhaps even later.[2] Without challenging the importance of the many other strands that lead into drama in the age of Shakespeare, we can nonetheless recognize that techniques discernible in early Elizabethan popular theater may lead us to more sophisticated versions of similar techniques in the plays that follow. An excursion into dramatic history can lay some helpful groundwork for the critic and the director.

Fortunately, this groundwork already has been provided by several scholars, particularly David Bevington.[3] In his suggestive introduction, Bevington observes that the unity and coherence of Elizabethan drama often have been obscured by the application of misleading criteria: "The fallacy of enforcing classical precept upon late medieval structure is not so much the invidious comparison of greater and lesser as it is confusion of incommensurate qualities. One cannot account for these plays by aesthetic laws of unity, correspondence, subordination, and

2. For example, Fulwell's *Like Will to Like* may have been performed at the Rose in 1600. See R. A. Foakes and R. T. Rickert, eds., *Henslowe's Diary* (Cambridge, 1961), p. 164.

3. From *"Mankind" to Marlowe: Growth of Structure in the Popular Drama of Tudor England* (Cambridge, Mass., 1962). For other relevant studies see the second section of the bibliography.

the like, because they were not composed with such ideas in mind. If some contemporary had had occasion to speak for the critically inarticulate authors of these plays, and had extracted a pattern or series of patterns from their work, he might have spoken quite differently of repetitive effect, multiplicity, episode, progressive theme." Bevington points out that the "critical spokesmen of the Renaissance—Sidney, Gosson, Jonson—were largely hostile to the native tradition," and concludes that "any explanatory theory must be supplied by an examination of the plays themselves." Before embarking upon his examination, he poses a question relevant both to the moralities and the later, more mature drama. If "coordination" rather than "subordination of one part to another" was to be the operative principle, "how was the drama to discover meaningful statement from a linear, episodic, and progressive sequence?" Such a drama of "coordination" (or "multiple unity") could be subject to many dangers (such as formlessness resulting from "unselective choice of episode"), but Bevington argues that "progressive sequence was not in itself incapable of coherent effect"[4] and backs up his argument with a thorough analysis of the popular canon of intermediate and late moralities and interludes.

Bevington's primary evidence comes from a group of plays published in the 1560s and 1570s, which were "offered for acting," thereby presumably designed for professional troupes of four or more actors and written with their limitations in mind. Usually included at the outset of the printed play is a cast list setting up the fifteen to thirty roles so that they can be handled by a limited number of actors adept at doubling and changing costume. Although the poetry in such plays rarely rises above banal mediocrity (and often sinks lower), Bevington demonstrates the considerable skill involved in sustaining the plots, the tempo, and even the illusion of a full stage (as in the trial scene of *All for Money*) with only four or five actors. Various

4. Ibid., p. 3.

working principles can be noted as basic to the dramaturgy (alternation of groups of figures, suppression of dramatis personae late in a play), so that in his final chapters Bevington can apply such inherited techniques to the plays of Marlowe.

Here then, in the period just before Marlowe and Shakespeare, existed a professional theater, with its own distinctive know-how, geared to a widely dispersed audience (which certainly did not disappear totally in 1576). Even with severe limitations upon personnel, props, and facilities, these plays could achieve "meaningful statement from a linear, episodic, and progressive sequence." The one possibility not explored by Bevington, however, is the visual dimension of such plays, particularly the use of visual analogues to link various elements or episodes in that sequence. Since few props could be carried (or borrowed) by a traveling troupe, the possible effects are quite limited, and the evidence is not as complete as we might wish (although the stage directions in a few of these plays are unusually informative about authorial intention). Yet, as Bevington demonstrates, the substantial theatrical expertise behind these plays often could offset their linguistic deficiencies. Such know-how, moreover, was there as a common fund at the birth of our great age of drama. Here is a likely point of departure for an investigation of Elizabethan drama and the viewer's eye.

As a starting point, let us call to mind the best-known prop in the late morality plays—the Vice's dagger of lath. Later references cite at least one standard bit of stage business associated with this prop. Thus, in *Twelfth Night*, Feste describes "the old Vice" who with his "dagger of lath, / In his rage and his wrath, / Cries, ah, ha! to the devil" (4. 2. 124–28). Similarly, in *1 Henry IV*, Falstaff threatens Hal: "If I do not beat thee out of thy kingdom with a dagger of lath, and drive all thy subjects afore thee like a flock of wild geese, I'll never wear hair on my face more" (2. 4. 136–39). The same stage business is recalled by Samuel Harsnet who describes "the old church plays, when the nimble Vice would skip up nimbly like a jackanapes into the devil's neck, and ride the devil a course, and belabour him with his wooden dagger, till he made him roar."[5] But, curiously, the extant moralities provide no clear examples of such a scene. In the comic interplay between the Vice (Sin) and Satan in Lupton's *All for Money*, there are threatened (and perhaps some actual) blows, but no specific indication that the dagger is used (although Sin is wearing one) and the Vice is not carried off by the Devil. The Vice *is* carried off at the end of Fulwell's *Like Will to Like* but again there is no explicit reference to a belaboring of Satan with a dagger.

These three relatively familiar references to the Vice's dagger, moreover, may have obscured other possibilities, for in several of the late moralities the prop may form part of a larger pattern not limited to a comic Devil. For example, in W. Wager's *Enough is as Good as a Feast*[6] the Vice (Covetous) establishes his supremacy over his vice lieutenants by the usual verbal and physical intimidation; although we cannot be sure how often or how lavishly the dagger is used, at least one stage direction tells us: *"He fighteth with them both with his dagger"* (440). This morality is devoted largely to the career of Worldly Man who, unlike his counterpart Heavenly Man, is not satisfied with Enough, chooses Covetous and his henchmen, and misuses his worldly possessions. By the end of the play, Worldly Man has so succumbed to the Vice's control that he can ignore the warning of the Prophet and go to sleep on stage. At this point, *"Enter God's Plague and stand behind him awhile before he speak"* (1222 s.d.); the long speech concludes:

> I am the plague of God properly called
> Which cometh on the wicked suddenly;

5. *A Declaration of egregious Popish Impostures* (London, 1603), pp. 114–15. I have modernized the spelling.
6. Text used for both *Enough* and *The Longer Thou Livest* is the RRD edition, ed. R. Mark Benbow (Lincoln, Neb., 1967).

> *I go through all towns and cities strongly walled,*
> *Striking to death, and that without all mercy.*
> *Here thou wicked, covetous person I do strike.*

[1243–47]

Later Worldly Man describes his dream: "And methought before me the Plague of God did stand / Ready to strike me with a sword in his hand" (1301–2). With the exception of the brief appearances of Heavenly Man, the bulk of this play has been concerned with the power of the Vice in this world, a power often represented by his dagger, but here, as elsewhere in the morality tradition, the final movement of the play presents that larger justice awaiting worldly men in the next world, a justice represented by the sword of God's Plague. The Vice's dagger therefore need not be an end in itself, a convenient device to elicit laughter or "good theater," but could be a lesser, worldly version of that greater sword or two-handed engine (an effect equivalent to the two sergeant scenes in *The Tide Tarrieth No Man*).

Even though explicit stage directions often are lacking, such a combination of dagger and sword (two portable and accessible props) can be found (or sensed) in enough extant plays to suggest it was a stock device. Thus in Fulwell's *Like Will to Like*[7] the Vice (Nichol Newfangle) has no vice lieutenants to intimidate, but early in the play does resort to threats and blows to establish his authority over two of his victims (Ralph Roister and Tom Tosspot). No dagger is mentioned at this point, but, since Nichol does have such a weapon, an actor surely would use it. Late in the play the same two victims, now stripped and degraded after their riotous living, turn on the Vice, beat him with their newly won beggar's tools, and appropriate the dagger of lath. Nichol describes the action:

7. W. Carew Hazlitt, ed., *A Select Collection of Old English Plays Originally Published by Robert Dodsley in the Year 1744*, 4th ed. (London, 1874), 3:303–59. Hereafter this edition will be cited as Dodsley.

Now am I driven to play the master of fence.
Come no near me, you knaves, for your life,
Lest I stick you both with this woodknife.
Back, I say! back, thou sturdy beggar!
Body of me, they have ta'en away my dagger.

[p. 350]

In the previous scene an alternative way of life had been commended when Virtuous Living, the figure who stands in opposition to the Vice, was awarded a sword and crown as his reward (p. 342). While Nichol, minus his weapon, lies groaning on the ground, moreover, the dramatist brings on stage his justice figure, Severity, who carries a sword as his major prop (pp. 351–53). Nichol is not completely subdued at this point (he temporarily joins forces with Severity to uncover two more offenders, Cuthbert Cutpurse and Pierce Pickpurse), but once again the failure of the Vice's power is juxtaposed with the rightful assertion of authority, and, as in *Enough*, the sword and dagger serve as visual reference points to heighten the viewer's awareness of a major theme.

Such interplay between true and false weapons need not be limited to the Vice's dagger of lath. Thus in Wager's *The Longer Thou Livest the More Fool Thou Art*, Moros's foolishness is displayed through his brandishing of the sword and dagger provided by Wrath. The latter's instructions ("draw thy dagger at every word"—832) are taken seriously by the foolish protagonist who states that "these weapons have set me on a fire" (835) and adds that "to be fighting now is all my desire" (837). Throughout a long scene, Moros flourishes his sword (835 s.d.), fights alone until he is out of breath, plays with his dagger, and boasts of what he will do to the virtues when they return, while the vices make acerbic comments (such as "He showeth the nature of a fool right, / Which is to chide and fight without a cause"—840–41). When Discipline does reappear, however, the stage direction tells us: "*Let Moros let fall his sword and hide him*" (948);

when Wrath and Idleness urge Moros to "take thy sword in thy hand" (962), the fool asks them to act for him ("Take you my sword and drive him hence"—967). In a similar situation later in the play, Moros asks the vices if he should draw his weapons against Discipline, but, in a broadly comic scene, first his dagger (1629) and then his sword (1653) are stuck and cannot be pulled forth. In the final stage of his career, Moros enters *"furiously with a grey beard"* (1742 s.d.) and again fights alone on stage (1752 s.d.), at which point the dramatist brings on God's Judgment *"with a terrible visure"* (1758 s.d.) and with a sword. In his continuing folly, Moros calls upon his followers to "bring your clubs, bills, bows and staves" to support him against this enemy (1773), but God's Judgment makes clear to the audience the efficacy of the higher power he represents:

> *I represent God's severe judgment,*
> *Which dallieth not where to strike he doth purpose.*
> *Hither am I sent to the punishment*
> *Of this impious fool, here called Moros*
> *Who hath said there is no God in his heart.*
> . . . .
> *For as much as vengeance to God doth belong*
> *And he will the same recompense,*
> *That he is a God of power, mighty and strong,*
> *The fools shall know by experience.*
> *With this sword of vengeance I strike thee.*
> Strike *Moros* and let him fall down
>
> [1763–67; 1787–91]

Here at the climax of the play a false or limited weapon, which (like the Vice's dagger of lath) hitherto has been a source of laughter, is juxtaposed with a truly potent weapon wielded by a figure who represents a higher power ignored by the foolish protagonist. The various references to the dangers of sharp "edge-tools" in the hands of a fool or madman (842–45, 1947–

50) further develop this distinction between weapons that are abused and that higher "sword of vengeance" that awaits erring humanity.

The most extensive use of the dagger and sword is to be found in *The Tide Tarrieth No Man*. Early in the play Courage controls his lieutenants through the typical threats and physical action; at one such moment Wapull directs: *"Out quickly with his dagger"* (200 s.d.). Midway in the play Courage strikes the courtier for "sport" (1120) although the manner of the blow (fist or dagger) is not specified; a bit later, the Vice and Hurtful Help fight *"to prolong the time"* (1214 s.d.) so that another actor can have time to make a difficult change in costume, but again the dagger is not cited. In contrast to the obvious power of Courage during the first two-thirds of this morality (expressed at least in part through the dagger), the audience is offered the spectacle of Christianity who should be exhibiting the well-known Pauline armor, but instead, owing to the wicked nature of the world, is "deformed" in appearance. As the elaborate stage direction tells us (1439): "Christianity *must enter with a sword, with a title of Policy, but on the other side of the title, must be written God's Word, also a shield, whereon must be written Riches, but on the other side of the shield must be Faith.*" During the scene that follows, Faithful Few turns the titles so that Faith and God's Word take their proper place, but moments later Christianity is forced to resume the burden of Riches and Policy because of the continued depravity of Greediness and the Vice. The restoration of the true sword and shield must wait until the very end of the play. Again Faithful Few is on stage, this time with Authority, who bears "this sword of God's power" (1837). When Correction tries to arrest the Vice (as described in chapter 1), Courage *"draweth his dagger and fighteth"* (1821 s.d.), once more attempting to assert his power. But the Vice's dagger, which earlier had dominated the action, now fails, physically and symbolically, when juxtaposed with the sword of God's authority and the correction that accompanies it. Once Courage has departed under arrest, more-over, Christianity's sword of Truth (and shield of Faith) can be restored to their pristine state by Faithful Few in the final action of the play. As in the other moralities cited, the dramatist's use of daggers and swords provides an audience with a visual pattern that reinforces the major themes and movements. Or, in Heywood's terms, lively action is the soul of this drama.

This treatment of daggers and swords in several Elizabethan moralities written for small troupes may seem like caviar to the general reader. But if we take into account the limited stage properties and, by extension, the limited visual effects possible for such troupes, we can recognize the expertise behind the use of weaponry *in bono* and *in malo*. Clearly, the two phases of such plays correspond neatly to the two sets of weapons—one associated with the temporary, worldly power of the Vice, the other with the higher powers invoked at the end of the action. The famous dagger of lath need not, any more than the Vice himself, have an autonomous identity independent of the original play, but rather can be seen as a meaningful part of a conventional pattern which in visual terms juxtaposes two disparate weapons for the edification of the audience. Here, even in the most rudimentary form of Elizabethan professional theater, is interesting evidence for meaningful staging and stagecraft directed at the viewer's eye.

This discussion, of course, need not be limited to swords and daggers. For example, consider the use of another easily accessible stage property, a chair, in at least two plays. Thus, early in *Like Will to Like* the Vice sits in a chair (p. 321) to judge whether Tom Tosspot or Ralph Roister deserves the promised patrimony (beggary). Moments later Hance, the drunken Fleming, sits in the chair (p. 327) and, after his evil-favored dance, sits down and falls asleep (p. 330). In obvious contrast, Virtuous Living is placed in the chair by Honor and God's Promises and presented with a sword and crown. Other scenes might have incorporated this chair, although specific evidence is lacking; at the least, a seated figure would catch the eye of the audience when the Vice rides off on the Devil's back (p. 357). Even with such relatively limited use of a chair, the differing paths of life presented by the play could be further clarified by comparable scenes built around a recurring stage property.

More elaborate use of a chair can be seen in the two most complex scenes of Thomas Lupton's *All for Money*.[8] When Money enters to begin the "genealogy of sin" sequence, the stage direction tells us, *"there must be a chair for him to sit in, and under it or near the same there must be some hollow place for one to come up in"* (202). After his initial speech, *"Money sitteth down in a chair"* (230 s.d.) and *"feigneth himself to be sick"* (248 s.d.). Then Lupton directs: *"Here Money shall make as though he would vomit, and with some fine conveyance Pleasure shall appear from beneath, and lie there appareled"* (l. 278 s.d.). Through the same "fine conveyance" Pleasure begets Sin who begets Damnation, with the chair as dramatic focus each time. In a subsequent scene Satan refers to his chair in Hell (530), but most of the scenes do not explicitly demand this stage property, whether for Judas and Dives in Hell or for Godly Admonition at the end. The exception is the most complex scene in the play in which the corrupt magistrate, All for Money, hears a series of petitioners while *"sitting in a chair"* (1000 s.d.). The proclamation establishes the kind of "justice" to be dispensed, for we are told that if petitioners "come from Money then they shall be heard quickly, / Be their matter never so wrong, they shall be sped and not tarry" (1011–12). The allegorical process set up earlier by which Money led to Sin and Damnation can be linked visually to this concrete demonstration of how Money can corrupt justice.

Visual analogues need not be limited to recurring stage properties. Thus *The Trial of Treasure*[9] presents the careers of two

8. Ed. Ernst Vogel, *Shakespeare Jahrbuch* 40 (1904): 129–86. I have modernized the spelling.
9. Dodsley, 3:257–301.

protagonists, Lust and Just, who confront each other in the opening scene and then follow their divergent paths toward damnation and salvation (much like Worldly Man and Heavenly Man). Through a variety of verbal and visual devices, the anonymous dramatist continually plays off one hero and his chosen way of life against the other. For example, in the third scene Just bridles the Vice, Inclination, and announces:

> *Thus should every man, that will be called Just,*
> *Bridle and subdue his beastly inclination,*
> *That he in the end may obtain perfect trust,*
> *The messenger of God to give sight to salvation.*

[p. 279]

Moments later, Lust unbridles the Vice (who has promised to lead him to Lady Treasure), thereby acting out his chosen path. In the final scene, after Lust literally and figuratively has been reduced to dust, Just can complete the pattern by bridling the Vice a second time.

A similar technique can be found in the center of the play. First Just appears with Trust, "*a woman plainly appareled*" wearing a crown (p. 283), and with Contentation to provide a lengthy analysis of "true trust" and "celestial treasure." This heavenly alternative is then countered by Lust's subsequent appearance with Treasure, "*a woman finely appareled*" (p. 288), and with Pleasure, who "will be always with Treasure in sight" (p. 291). Since Trust and Treasure are the only female figures to appear during this play, the analogy between them as allegorical goals could be theatrically emphatic, particularly with parallel blocking of the two scenes; the analogy would also hold for their attendant satisfactions, Pleasure and Contentation. Certainly this anonymous dramatist never passes up an opportunity to make his point clear. So the Vice observes:

> *Marry, now you are well indeed, Master Lust;*
> *This is better, I trow, than the life of the just:*

> *They be compelled to possess contentation,*
> *Having no treasure but trust of salvation.*

[p. 290]

But verbal homiletics like this can be enhanced by careful use of visually analogous figures, stage groupings, and stage business in consecutive scenes. In spite of an apparent lack of artistic sophistication, here is a fruitful dramaturgical pattern whereby two figures, whether Just and Lust or Hal and Hotspur, can be played off against each other in a manner evident to the eye as well as the ear of the spectator.

Such consideration of the parallel figures in *The Trial of Treasure* leads to the larger question of how costumes, stage groupings, and even exits and entrances can provide added coherence to an episodic, linear sequence of dramatic events. Unfortunately, in both the late moralities and the drama that follows it is much easier to document the use of props than to establish convincingly the existence of other visual patterns. But consider again *Enough is as Good as a Feast*. At the end of the first scene, Worldly Man, described by Wager as *"stout and frolic"* (92 s.d.), is temporarily converted to the path of virtue and exits with Contentation and Heavenly Man (who is dressed simply, perhaps as a clergyman). Heavenly Man's final line ("Give me your hand, then together let us depart"—279) sets up the stage picture of a well-dressed, worldly figure exiting arm in arm with a plainer figure of virtue (with a third supporting figure perhaps following). When Worldly Man reappears, he is clad *"in a strange attire"* (627 s.d.), perhaps a penitential garment, and is accompanied by Enough, who is *"poorly arrayed"* (636) and is described by the vices and later by Worldly Man himself as a "beggarly knave." During the scene, Enough exits alone, having been rejected by Worldly Man, who has chosen instead Covetous, the Vice, and Precipitation. As the protagonist is about to leave the stage with the two vices, Covetous says: "By the mass, give me your hand. / Come, go with me; let us no longer idle stand"

(947–48). Since the Vice is now wearing a cap, a gown, a chain, and perhaps a cloak, for a second time the audience would see a well-dressed, prosperous figure (Worldly Man, Covetous) exiting arm in arm with a simply or strangely attired figure (Heavenly Man, Worldly Man) while accompanied in some unspecified way by yet a third figure (Contentation, Precipitation). Similar blocking could call attention to the analogue, while the differences between the two exits could heighten the stages in Worldly Man's career.

Subsequent scenes in this play set up similar distinctions based upon contrasts in costume. For example, the Tenant, the Servant, and the Hireling, who complain bitterly about Worldly Man's oppression, are dressed simply, even *"poorly"* (992 s.d. for the Servant), while the subject of their complaints appears for the third time *"all brave"* (1112 s.d.); this well-dressed figure, however, eventually is struck down by God's Plague and carried off on Satan's back (1471 s.d.). In contrast, the final scene brings on Heavenly Man, Contentation, and Enough in their simple garb praising the life content with enough, while the final figure to appear is Rest who announces that "with joys I am adorned, yea on every side" (1525), joys that God has sent to Heavenly Man (1529–30). Although the stage business is unclear, Heavenly Man receives something here (perhaps a crown or a wreath) and exits with some positive, permanent reward (perhaps arm in arm with Rest) in sharp contrast to his worldly counterpart whose brave trappings led only to an ignominious departure on Satan's back. Again the homily can be given considerable theatrical force through the visual language of costumes and exits.

My examples from the late moralities are intended to be illustrative, not exhaustive; indeed, I have not drawn upon better-known troupe plays like *Cambises* and *Horestes*. Nevertheless, critics and directors not concerned with dramatic history may not be enthusiastic about a demonstration of increased coherence or dramatic integrity in such plays, for the presence of techniques directed at the viewer's eye certainly does not transform the homiletics of Wapull, Lupton, Wager, and Fulwell into great dramatic art. But, having learned that such know-how was available at this early stage in the development of Elizabethan drama, we have every reason to expect equivalent effects in later plays by dramatists faced with similar audiences and analogous formal problems. In fact, the modern reader should be surprised *not* to find evidence of staging and stagecraft for the viewer's eye, whether in major plays or in those plays that lack Kyd's rhetoric or Marlowe's mighty line and therefore might gain added coherence from their theatrical dimension.

In subsequent chapters I will explore the possibilities in the age of Shakespeare. For now, a few brief links will suffice. Thus the reader aware of the use of a readily available prop like the chair, as in *All for Money* and *Like Will to Like*, would not be surprised to find Marlowe in *Doctor Faustus* building a series of scenes around chairs and thrones, a sequence (especially Faustus's bargain with the horse-courser) that helps to chart the progression of the protagonist. Dekker and Jonson may not have known *The Trial of Treasure*, but both could resort to the same technique whereby a Lady Trust could be contrasted to a Lady Treasure to stress alternative ways of life. Thus, in act 4, scene 2, of *Patient Grissil* we see the title figure back in her garb of poverty, while in the next scene the proud, tempestuous Gwenthyan takes on beggar's garb, not to show humility but to embarrass Sir Owen in front of the marquess. As in *The Trial of Treasure*, a figure on stage spells out the contrast; thus Marquess Gwalter says in an aside: "Oh my dear Grissil, how much different / Art thou to this curst spirit here, I see / My Grissil's virtues shine"[10] (4. 3. 156–58). Similarly, in act 4 of *Bartholomew Fair* first Grace Wellborn (4. 3) and then Win Littlewit (4. 5) are

10. Here and in subsequent chapters, all quotations from Dekker are taken from Fredson Bowers, ed., *The Dramatic Works of Thomas Dekker*, 4 vols. (Cambridge, 1953–1961). I have modernized the spelling.

alone on stage with two men who contend for them; Grace controls her situation, pacifying Quarlous and Winwife, while Win is easily seduced by Whit and Knockem into becoming a green woman.

For an equivalent to Wapull's use of a distinctive costume, that of the sergeant, we can note another Jonsonian example whereby the disguise of a Spanish don is used to link two moments in *The Alchemist*.[11] To uncover the truth about Face, Subtle, and Doll, the shrewd Surly in act 4 poses as a potential customer, Don Diego, and succeeds in gulling the gullers; thus in scene 6 he can tell the truth to Dame Pliant, knock down Subtle, and threaten to bring down the entire house of cards. But Face is equal to the occasion, rallying Kastril, Drugger, and Ananias to create an uproar of fools and rascals that drives Surly, his truth, and his Spanish costume offstage. The first figure to wear this distinctive costume has tried to control the activities of the rogues and failed. But in act 5 it is Lovewit who appears in the Spanish ruff and cloak (5. 5. 8), not for retribution or ordering or education but to cash in on the spoils available, thanks to the venture tripartite, particularly the wealthy, attractive widow whom he has just married. Instead of opposing Face (as had Surly), this version of a Spanish don accepts the shrewdest of the conspirators as his "brain," later adding: "I will be rul'd by thee in anything, Jeremy" (5. 5. 7, 143). The two uses of this distinctive costume thereby can set up a revealing contrast between the goals and successes of these two figures, Surly and Lovewit, that forms an important part of Jonson's ironic climax. Yet the technique is not far removed from that found in the late moralities, whether in Wapull's sergeants or in the Vice's dagger which is countered by the rightful sword of authority.

To develop further such visual contrasts and analogues is the purpose of the next chapter. At this point, let me recall Beckerman's formulation cited earlier. Obviously, spectacles com-

11. Text used is the Revels editions, ed. F. H. Mares (London, 1967).

pacted of acknowledged and unacknowledged preconceptions stand between us and Elizabethan drama. If indeed we wish to adjust our spectacles to see the plays more clearly, we should not ignore the problems facing the early Elizabethan dramatists or, even more important, some of the theatrical answers to the problems already in practice before the arrival of Kyd, Marlowe, Greene, and Shakespeare. To blink at such evidence is to satisfy modern tastes at the expense of a larger, more revealing perspective, for in curious yet revealing ways the staging and stagecraft found in these late moralities provide a valuable springboard into the far greater plays that follow.

Chapter 3

Linking Analogues

The particularly restrictive conditions faced by dramatists and players produced a distinctive stagecraft and structure in the late moralities. Once such conditions ceased to exist, however (at least around London), changes in structure and technique could be expected; for example, plays could become longer and more complex when twelve or more actors (including at least two boys to play female roles) could be used rather than four or five (or even the eight designated in *Cambises*). After 1576 permanent theaters provided not only a familiar acting area but also a home for more extensive properties, costumes, and appurtenances that no longer needed to be portable (as suggested by Henslowe's inventory of 1598). We can therefore expect considerable advances on all theatrical fronts in the age of Shakespeare.

Nonetheless, improvements in facilities and resources cannot in themselves resolve the problem of sequential form posed by Bevington. If the action in mature Elizabethan drama (for example, in the history plays) continues to be multiple, varied, and episodic, there is no reason to assume that Shakespeare and his contemporaries would have scorned the legacy of theatrical expertise bequeathed by Wager, Lupton, Wapull, and Fulwell. The purpose of this chapter is to consider one answer to the problem of sequential form provided by the late morality dramatists—the use of analogues for the viewer's eye to link disparate moments in the dramatic action.

Such analogues fall roughly into two categories. First, as

seen with Trust and Treasure (along with Contentation and Pleasure) in *The Trial of Treasure*, is the short-term analogue that occurs within a brief period of dramatic time; such a short-term effect is well suited to comparison and contrast (in that instance to spell out the divergent paths of Just and Lust). At the other end of the spectrum is the visual analogue spaced over a wider expanse of dramatic time; when perceived, such a linking device could provide a larger sense of structure for an entire action. Thus, in the late moralities, the overall movement of a play could be emphasized when the Vice's dagger of lath, in evidence throughout much of the action, is contrasted to the sword of God's authority, visible only at the end; similarly, the two sergeant-prisoner scenes of *The Tide Tarrieth No Man* could bring into focus the two phases of the allegory. The bridling, unbridling, and rebridling of Inclination in *The Trial of Treasure* could provide a sense of patterned development as could the two chair scenes in *All for Money* or the costumes and exits in *Enough*. In all such cases, linkages for the eye help to clarify the dramatist's essential points for the viewer in the theater.

The short-term visual analogue, easier to spot and to interpret, can serve as a good point of departure. An excellent example is provided by two consecutive scenes in *The Tempest*, act 2, scene 2, and act 3, scene 1. In the first, the stage direction has Caliban enter *"with a burthen of wood"*; in the second, less than two hundred lines later, the stage direction has Ferdinand enter *"bearing a log."* Critics may disagree about Shakespeare's purpose in establishing such an obvious link. Certainly the connection shows something about the issues of freedom and service orchestrated throughout the play, especially since Caliban soon throws off his burden to follow Stephano while Ferdinand endures his "wooden slavery" and earns Miranda. But regardless of the exact interpretation by critic or director, a link has been established for the eye between two disparate figures who are taking different routes that lead to quite different rewards, a link that helps to structure the experience of the viewer.

The short-term analogue is particularly effective at linking episodes or figures from two independent plots. The more disparate the figures or plots, moreover, the more striking is the effect. In *The Changeling*, for example, several scenes set up parallels between DeFlores and Lollio (or between Alsemero and Alibius) in order to stress the contrast between Beatrice Joanna and Isabella. In act 3, scene 3, Lollio, who has overheard Antonio's wooing of Isabella, tries to use that knowledge for sexual blackmail only to be resisted by his quarry and interrupted by the arrival of Alibius. In the next scene, the heart of the tragedy, DeFlores succeeds in his sexual blackmail of Beatrice Joanna because she, unlike Isabella, has become "the deed's creature." Here as elsewhere in the play, a combination of similar stagings along with disparate results could heighten the revealing links between the two plots. Again, in act 5 of *Volpone*, Jonson links his subplot to his main action by showing how two different figures literally can descend to the level of animals. Thus Sir Politick Would-be's descent, so that he can crawl about the stage in his tortoise's shell (while Peregrine and others stand over and control him) is followed moments later by Voltore's equivalent action during the sham dispossession wherein the formerly impressive advocate is reduced to a writhing, contorted figure on the floor of the stage (while this time Volpone, not Peregrine, stands over him, exerting his control). In high comic terms, both scenes use the same striking physical actions and the same blocking to enact the depths to which men can descend when their reason is clouded or overwhelmed by baser forces.

As usual, the absence of adequate stage directions prevents any authoritative claims about such scenes, but without straining the evidence many possibilities exist to enhance relationships already cited by critics. In act 2, scene 4, of *Cymbeline*, for example, Posthumus rejects the reasoned caution of Philario and instead accepts the slanders of the villainous Jachimo. Moments later in act 3, scene 1, Cymbeline rejects Lucius and the bond to Rome and instead accepts the position espoused by his evil queen and the foolish Cloten. Parallel blocking easily could call attention to the links between the two choosers. The well-known double plot in *Friar Bacon and Friar Bungay*[1] provides several possibilities. Thus, after the four deaths of the Lamberts and Serlsbys (deaths associated both with Bacon's magic and Margaret's beauty), Friar Bacon breaks his glass and exits, announcing to Bungay that he will "spend the remnant of my life / In pure devotion, praying to my God / That he would save what Bacon vainly lost" (scene 13, lines 106–8). A director need only have Bacon at this point shed his magician's garb (perhaps to reveal a penitential garment beneath) to have a firm visual parallel to the stage direction that follows immediately: "*Enter Margaret in nun's apparel.*"

Perhaps the most interesting use of the short-term analogue is to be found in *1 Henry IV* where, at the outset, Shakespeare sets up a series of such moments so that an audience will have the opportunity to contrast Hal and Hotspur. Thus in our first view of the prince (1. 2.) we see two figures on stage (a youth and an old man) with a third figure (Poins) arriving with a plot (the Gadshill robbery). Moments later in the next scene, after the angry departure of the king, the audience sees again a youth and an old man, this time Hotspur and Northumberland rather than Hal and Falstaff, while again a third figure (this time Worcester rather than Poins) enters with a plot (against the king's crown rather than the king's crowns). Parallel staging of this early analogue could set up a series of comparisons and contrasts between these two young men, an effect that could help to structure the entire play.[2] Consider, for example, the

1. Text used is the RRD edition, ed. Daniel Seltzer (Lincoln, Neb., 1963).
2. Such structural use of two contrasting heroes can be noted in several other Elizabethan historical plays (for example, George Peele's *The Battle of Alcazar*, Thomas Lodge's *The Wounds of Civil War*, the anonymous *Life and Death of Jack Straw*) and may be an outgrowth of the late moralities like *The Trial of Treasure*. For a more extensive treatment of this question, see Alan C. Dessen,

stage images at the beginnings of act 2, scene 3, and act 2, scene 4. In the former, an impetuous, impolitic Hotspur, with a letter in his hand, rejects the analysis provided by a cautious lord, an analysis that proves accurate by the end of the play. About a hundred lines later, at the outset of the famous tavern scene, Prince Hal describes the honor he has gained in *his* recent action (drinking with the lads of Eastcheap) and tells of the new language he has learned ("dyeing scarlet," "play it off," "hem!"). To establish a clear analogy to Hotspur and his letter, the prince need only brandish a piece of paper upon which he has recorded his philological finds or the pennyworth of sugar supplied by Francis the drawer. Through such a contrast, Shakespeare is playing off Hotspur's inability to learn from others against Hal's ability to master and use the languages (and assumptions) of those around him, including Henry IV and Falstaff (as suggested at the end of the tavern scene when the prince stands over the sleeping knight with the paper from Falstaff's pocket in his hand).

Although the short-term analogues may be easier to recognize and explain, those spaced over a wider expanse of dramatic time are of greater importance for this study. Rather than setting up quick, deft contrasts (Caliban versus Ferdinand, Hal versus Hotspur) or parallels (Margaret and Bacon, Voltore and Sir Pol), the long-term analogues can serve a wide variety of purposes: marking phases in the development of a protagonist; linking analogous moments in separate plots; setting up important dramatic ironies. With justification, critics have called our attention to verbal and thematic repetitions in Elizabethan drama, so there is every reason to assume that equivalent iterative effects may exist for the viewer's eye. Ideally, verbal, visual, and thematic materials should combine to establish that larger theatrical effect for which the dramatist and the actors are striving.

"The Intemperate Knight and the Politic Prince: Late Morality Structure in *1 Henry IV*," *Shakespeare Studies* 7 (1974): 147–71.

Let me start with a classic example. By now surely every reader is aware that the Gadshill robbery in *1 Henry IV* bears *some* relation to the main plot rebellion that climaxes at Shrewsbury. But does the relationship exist solely on an abstract (or "spatial") plane, available only to a kind of retrospective reasoning process? Or can this link be established for an attentive audience through a performance of the play? Consider first the robbery scene. After the merchants have been robbed by the four figures (Falstaff, Gadshill, Peto, and Bardolph), the stage direction reads: *"As they are sharing, the Prince and Poins set upon them"* (2. 2. 101 s.d.); when interrupted by Hal and Poins, the four thieves somehow are dividing up the spoils, probably grouped around their loot, which is laid out in front of them. A few scenes later (3. 1.) Shakespeare again brings on stage four figures (Hotspur, Glendower, Worcester, and Mortimer) who again are grouped around an object of common interest (this time a map of England) and who again are dividing up the spoils (this time the kingdom itself). A director easily could block these scenes so that the analogy would be emphatically clear. The result would be a link for the viewer's eye between two seemingly disparate actions which, we soon realize, are not as disparate as they first appear. There is, of course, much more to the analogy; thus the rerobbing by Prince Hal at Gadshill sets up his equivalent role in putting down Hotspur, as suggested by the latter's dying comment—"O Harry, thou hast robb'd me of my youth!" (5. 4. 77). But my primary concern here is with the striking visual analogy between act 2, scene 2, and act 3, scene 1, a linkage for the eye that could make quite clear to the viewer a relationship that easily could elude the reader faced only with the printed page.

Few widely spaced analogues are this clear, largely because of the absence of adequate stage directions or external evidence. But once the potential is recognized, many otherwise inexplicable moments or details begin to make excellent sense. For example, editors and critics of *Edward II*[3] have puzzled over the presence of a "horseboy" during the scene in which Gaveston is captured by the barons and then sent off in Pembroke's custody. One recent editor (Roma Gill) eliminates the speech prefix entirely, giving the horseboy's one line to Pembroke; most editors reprint the prefix and line with no explanation. But consider the passage as a whole, especially the potential stage image. The barons are about to execute Gaveston when they are confronted with Edward II's request, conveyed by Arundel, to see his friend one last time. After some debate, the barons honor Pembroke's pledge to comply with this request and then bring Gaveston back; they depart leaving on stage Pembroke, Arundel, Gaveston, and Pembroke's men. After Pembroke invites Arundel to his house and the invitation is accepted, the text reads:

PEMBROKE: *So my lord. Come hither James;*
I do commit this Gaveston to thee;
Be thou this night his keeper; in the morning
We will discharge thee of thy charge; be gone.
GAVESTON: *Unhappy Gaveston, whither goest thou now?*
Exit cum seruis Pen.
HORSE BOY: *My lord, we'll quickly be at Cobham.*
Exeunt ambo.

[2. 5. 107–12]

The stage direction then follows immediately: "*Enter* Gaveston *mourning, and the* Earl of Pembroke's *men.*" Within a few lines Warwick and his company enter to reject James's pleas and to whisk away Gaveston to his death; James can only comment: "Come fellows, it booted not for us to strive; / We will in haste go certify our lord" (3. 1. 19–20).

3. Text used is the New Mermaid edition, ed. W. Moelwyn Merchant (New York, 1968). I have also looked at the handling of the horseboy passage by other recent editors of the play (Irving Ribner, Roma Gill, Fredson Bowers). For the passage from act 2, scene 5, I have used the original stage directions rather than the modernization by Merchant.

Of the many difficulties here, at least some result from modern assumptions about realism. Admittedly, the stage directions are puzzling; surely Pembroke and Arundel leave the stage together (*"ambo"*), while Gaveston departs with James and his retinue. But why does Marlowe in his text call attention to the horseboy who is not otherwise mentioned and indeed would have disappeared entirely from the play (as we now have it) were it not for this one speech prefix? If we can suspend for a moment the logic of realism, consider the possibility that the otherwise unidentified James, in spite of the responsibility entrusted to him, is not Pembroke's senior retainer but is rather a youth dressed in a riding outfit; the horseboy's line then would be a parting address to his master as James follows Gaveston and the other servants offstage, with Pembroke and Arundel leaving by another stage door. Indeed, the formal exit of the larger party need not be completed, for Gaveston's group could go to a stage door, start to depart, and then return quickly, as if pursued by Warwick's men. It then would be a James attired as a horseboy or some equivalent who vainly tries to protect Gaveston and must stand by helplessly when a superior force takes away his charge.

My purpose in belaboring the stage image presented by this episode becomes clear when one turns to the similar situation facing the other boy in the play, Edward III (who might have been played by the same child actor). At the end of the coronation scene, Mortimer's soldiers bring in as their prisoner the Earl of Kent who has been captured while trying to help Edward II escape. In spite of the pleas of the newly crowned king, Mortimer sentences Kent to death; the stage direction reads: *"They hale Edmund Earl of Kent away, and carry him to be beheaded."* The dialogue then reads:

KING: *What safety may I look for at his hands*
If that my uncle shall be murthered thus?
QUEEN: *Fear not, sweet boy, I'll guard thee from thy foes;*

> *Had Edmund lived, he would have sought thy death.*
> *Come, son, we'll ride ahunting in the park.*
> KING: *And shall my uncle Edmund ride with us?*
> QUEEN: *He is a traitor, think not on him; come.*

[5. 4. 108–14]

Here Edward III, rather than James, stands by powerlessly while Mortimer, rather than Warwick, takes away by force Kent, rather than Gaveston, to his death (with Edward II's death in the next scene a further development in the same direction). To heighten the link for the eye, a director need only have an attendant (or the queen herself) take off the young king's regalia during the speeches above and supply a riding costume, even a crop. An audience thereby would be presented with visual evidence of a recurring pattern whereby specious claims about the good of the monarch and the realm (as iterated by the barons, Warwick, and now Mortimer) consistently can override honor, loyalty, and simple justice; on a deeper level, Marlowe is exploring the image of the king as a rider who cannot yet control his horse of state. To one kind of logic, the entrusting of an important political prisoner to a horseboy makes little sense, but, if the stage imagery of these two scenes is analogous, a larger theatrical logic could set up a potent effect. What at first appears to be an excrescent moment midway in the action could turn out to be both a foreshadowing of and a revealing key to a major moment in this rich, complex play.

Such foreshadowing through visual analogues can produce a variety of effects. For example, Benvolio's unsuccessful attempt in the opening scene of *Romeo and Juliet* to part the fighting servants, a peacemaking effort that only leads to a bout with Tybalt, prepares us in some way for Romeo's analogous effort in act 3, scene 1, when he tries to part Mercutio and Tybalt but only succeeds in bringing on the death of his friend and the fatal duel. The visual repetition here, easily enhanced through parallel staging, could heighten the star-crossed fates of the young people in this tragedy or could reinforce a sense of hatred and violence that cannot be controlled. Or, for a complex example of foreshadowing and linking, consider a play not noted for its tightly knit structure—John Webster's *The White Devil*.[4] In act 2, scene 2, the conjurer provides Bracciano and the audience with a vision in dumb show of the murders of Isabella and Camillo. As the stage direction tells us, first Dr. Julio poisons the portrait of Bracciano; then Isabella *"kneels down as to prayers, then draws the curtain of the picture, does three reverences to it, and kisses it thrice, she faints and will not suffer them to come near it, dies."* Before our eyes Isabella dies of a poisoned kiss. Her death is avenged in act 5 when Bracciano too is poisoned. There, moreover, the stage direction tells us that "Lodovico *sprinkles* Bracciano's *beaver with a poison"* (5. 2. 76 s.d.) so that the portion of the helmet closest to Bracciano's mouth receives the poison. The victim himself emphasizes the link when he exclaims to Vittoria: "Do not kiss me, for I shall poison thee" (5. 3. 26). Here, in a tragedy that grows out of a poisoned and self-destructive love, Webster links two visually provocative poisonings not so much as cause and effect (although such a relationship might be traced) but in a larger symbolic vein that adds coherence and meaning to the total effect. Since both Isabella and Bracciano in their respective scenes are accompanied by others (with their son Giovanni present each time), their anguish easily could be staged in parallel fashion. Even in a tragedy best known for its intense yet discrete dramatic moments, linking analogues are both possible and fruitful.

    For a similar example we can return to *Edward II*. After the king and Gaveston have been reunited at the outset of the play,

4. Text used is the Revels edition, ed. John Russell Brown (London, 1960). It is also possible, although certainly not provable, that Camillo's vaulting which leads to his death may somehow prefigure Bracciano's demise, especially if the dumb show of act 2 is linked visually either to the tournament or the strangling of act 5.

the Bishop of Coventry, who had played a major role in the favorite's exile, comes on stage promising to incense Parliament again. Although the exact stage business is unclear, the king directs Gaveston to "throw off his golden mitre, rend his stole, / And in the channel christen him anew," while Kent pleads with his brother ("lay not violent hands on him") and Gaveston talks of revenge (1. 1. 186–91). Before our eyes, an elaborately attired symbol of the religion that gives the king his legitimacy is being mocked, stripped, degraded, and "christened" with filthy water by two figures who take sardonic pleasure in the act. Later in the play Edward II himself, rather than the Bishop of Coventry, is degraded by two figures, Matrevis and Gurney; when the king asks for water, he too is offered "channel water" and seemingly threatened, so that he responds: "Traitors away, what, will you murther me, / Or choke your sovereign with puddle water?" (5. 3. 27–30). Edward's struggles are ineffectual, for the stage direction reads: *They wash him with puddle water, and shave his beard away.* The staging here has obvious symbolic value, especially as an inversion of the anointing of a king, an act of unkinging linked to what Edward has done to himself and to his office. But if the staging also echoes the analogous treatment of the Bishop of Coventry, a more specific link may be forged between Edward's degradation of a figure who should have been a support to his crown and the king's similar degradation here. Kent, moreover, who had stood by helplessly in the earlier scene, also appears here only to be arrested and taken away to his fateful final meeting with Mortimer. As in *The White Devil*, such an analogue, once perceived, can suggest a symbolic cause and effect whereby the earlier action against the bishop condoned by Edward II somehow has led to his helplessness here at the hands of two tormenters who act out a role visually analogous to that of the king and Gaveston in act 1. Such a link could heighten for the viewer Edward's own contribution to his present degradation, a responsibility he himself is not prepared to admit.

In a variety of ways linking analogues can help the viewer to see larger patterns or relationships. Of particular interest in this connection is the way in which such analogues can help to orchestrate the ethical problems associated with revenge. Consider first *Antonio's Revenge*,[5] certainly one of the least impressive of the revenge plays. The opening stage direction reads: "*Enter* Piero *unbrac'd, his arms bare, smear'd in blood, a poniard in one hand, bloody, and a torch in the other*"; this bloody villain then proceeds to gloat over the murders he has just committed and to celebrate his depravity. But at the end of act 3, scene 1, the hero of the play, Antonio, as the first step in his revenge, kills Julio, Piero's innocent son, while offering the audience such statements as: "Lo, thus I heave my blood-dyed hands to heaven; / Even like insatiate hell, still crying: 'More! / My heart hath thirsting dropsies after gore'" (211–13). When moments later the revenger appears, the stage direction reads: "*Enter* Antonio, *his arms bloody, in one hand a torch and in the other a poniard*" (3. 2. 75 s.d.). The visual link between Piero in act 1 and Antonio in act 3 is firm and obvious and raises questions about the stature of our hero-revenger when for a striking moment he stands before us as a duplication or reincarnation of his bloody antagonist. By first establishing Piero as the epitome of total villainy, Marston can demonstrate through this analogue how a noble yet passionate hero can degenerate to a level where he cannot readily be distinguished from the figure to whom he is opposed.

In other revenge plays this device can be equally striking and more meaningful. Outside of Shakespeare's plays the best example is to be found in *The Revenger's Tragedy*[6] where the

5. Text used is the RRD edition, ed. G. K. Hunter (Lincoln, Neb., 1965). I am aware of but in disagreement with the argument that *Antonio's Revenge* is a parody or burlesque of the revenge play. See, for example, R. A. Foakes, "John Marston's Fantastical Plays: *Antonio and Mellida* and *Antonio's Revenge*," *Philological Quarterly* 41 (1962): 229–39. For this and related reasons, however, I have avoided, for the most part, using examples from plays designed primarily for the child actors.

6. Text used is the RRD edition, ed. Lawrence J. Ross (Lincoln, Neb., 1966).

dramatist consistently uses short-term analogues to set up contrasts and parallels between two sets of brothers or two sets of revengers. For example, within a brief span of time in act 4 both sets of brothers are shown with drawn swords in the presence of their mothers: Vindice and Hippolito succeed in reforming Gratiana, while Ambitioso and Supervacuo have no effect upon the duchess. The six scenes that constitute act 3 establish a more elaborate contrast. Five of these scenes are devoted largely to the abortive plotting of Ambitioso and Supervacuo against their enemy (Lussurioso), which only succeeds in bringing about the death of their younger brother whom they were trying to save. In contrast, Vindice and Hippolito in the long and crucial act 3, scene 5, *do* destroy their enemy (the old duke) in a protracted and sadistic fashion. The dramatist further develops his ironic contrast in visual terms by having Gloriana's skull, Vindice's instrument for poisoning the duke, echoed in act 3, scene 6, by the head of the youngest son, which is handed to the other two would-be murderers.

But given the possibilities suggested in *Antonio's Revenge*, the most interesting link is displayed by the masques and murders of act 5. In acts 3 and 4 the emphasis had been upon the contrast between two sets of brothers (although the contrast could be muted if emphasis is placed upon the sadism and horror in the murder of the old duke). Yet in act 5, scene 3, Lussurioso and his three lords are killed by the first set of four masquers (Vindice and his allies) who have carefully copied the costumes of the next group of four, *"the other masque of intended murderers"* (48 s.d.), who enter a moment later looking for the same victims. The visual equation between the two groups had been stressed before the event when Vindice had instructed his cohorts "to take pattern / Of all those suits, the color, trimming, fashion, / E'en to an undistinguish'd hair almost" (5. 2. 15–17). For the eye of the viewer there can be no distinction between Vindice's group of masked murderers and Ambitioso's group, whether in costume or in action. The hero-revenger, who had pitted himself against the obvious corruption of the court in the opening scene, here has become visually indistinguishable from his enemies, and the carnage inflicted by both groups stresses their kinship. Vindice, of course, recognizes no such descent in himself, hence his amazement at Antonio's reaction to his confession. But through a series of visual links the dramatist has suggested the diminishing distance between Vindice and his antagonists and then provided this clear equation at the climax of the tragedy to make the point theatrically obvious.

To no one's surprise, the best example of this device is to be found in *Hamlet*, where a particularly striking analogue stands at the center of the play. Although almost every moment in this tragedy is rich with implications and possibilities, the first part of the player's speech devoted to Pyrrhus and Priam is of particular importance for establishing an ethical context for the question of revenge. Pyrrhus, we should remember, is described (in the passage declaimed by Hamlet) as the archetypal dire revenger—"hellish," covered "with blood of fathers, mothers, daughters, sons," "roasted in wrath and fire," and "o'er-sized with coagulate gore." Eventually, we are told, he makes "malicious sport" by "mincing with his sword" Priam's limbs (2. 2. 456–64, 513–14). Although no stage directions are provided, the player may not only be declaiming his lines but also miming Pyrrhus's actions as he stands over the helpless Priam. The only necessary prop would be a sword in the actor's hand, a weapon that could be supplied from the luggage of the troupe or, to stress a potential analogue, could be borrowed from Hamlet himself.

The behavior of the player-Pyrrhus is then carefully established by the text.

> for lo his sword,
> Which was declining on the milky head
> Of reverent Priam, seem'd i' th' air to stick.

> *So as a painted tyrant Pyrrhus stood*
> *And, like a neutral to his will and matter,*
> *Did nothing.*

[477–82]

This highly theatrical image of the revenger with sword poised in the air is sustained for over ten lines until

> *after Pyrrhus' pause*
> *A roused vengeance sets him new a-work,*
> *And never did the Cyclops' hammers fall*
> *On Mars's armor forg'd for proof eterne*
> *With less remorse than Pyrrhus' bleeding sword*
> *Now falls on Priam.*

[487–92]

For me, both the "for lo" of line 477 and the "Now" of line 492 demand appropriate action with a sword, first the pause with sword in air, then the swift descent to mince Priam's limbs. By introducing only one prop, a director could provide, in addition to the words themselves, a total dramatic image of the revenger in action, a staging that would enable the viewer to hear *and* see Pyrrhus's action which denies all sympathy to the act of revenge.

Once this stage image is established, the visual analogy to the prayer scene (3. 3.) is readily apparent. Here Hamlet, not Pyrrhus, stands over Claudius, not Priam, but visually the parallel could be quite clear, especially if the actors and director perceive the analogy and use similar blocking and gestures to heighten it. Again, the text firmly supports the parallel. Thus, Hamlet's initial reaction to the sight of the kneeling, oblivious king has all the trappings of purposeful revenge ("Now might I do it pat, now 'a is a-praying; / And now I'll do't"). But this forthright statement immediately is followed by Hamlet's version of Pyrrhus's pause ("That would be scann'd"). For reasons that have horrified Dr. Johnson and many subsequent readers, the hero concludes: "Up, sword, and know thou a more horrid hent"; a moment for revenge must be chosen "that has no relish of salvation in't." Like Pyrrhus, Hamlet has raised his sword over his enemy and then paused with that sword in midair. Granted, the hero now either sheathes the sword or carries it offstage in his hand, thereby (for the moment) differentiating himself from the hellish, bloody revenger of act 2. But for many readers and viewers, Hamlet's stated reason for putting up his sword (the desire for the damnation as well as the death of his enemy) seems as black and hellish as Pyrrhus's motives; the distinction between the two, moreover, may be short-lived, for in the next scene the hero *does* use his sword, making his pass through the arras to kill Polonius.

In all three of these revenge plays, the dramatists could use linking analogues to establish suggestive relationships for the viewer's eye, relationships that should give *us* pause. Whether the critic concludes that the link calls attention to the similarity or to the contrast between Hamlet and Pyrrhus, Shakespeare has set up a constant (Pyrrhus) in an earlier movement of his play (much like Piero or the evil brothers) and then played off his protagonist (much like Antonio or Vindice) against that constant through this emphatic theatrical technique. Much more remains to be said about the nature of Hamlet's (or Vindice's) revenge,[7] but such a striking analogy between the protagonist and a figure who should be his moral antithesis could have a substantial effect upon the viewer.

Such analogues linking the protagonist to some lesser figure are not, of course, limited to revenge plays. For example, there are various ways of staging the last two acts of *Othello* to establish a visual equation between Othello and Roderigo. In the ocular proof scene (4. 1.) the Moor is coached by Iago and then eavesdrops upon Iago and Cassio from some vantage point. Later in act 5, scene 1, Roderigo is also coached by Iago, who

7. For a more detailed treatment of revenge in *Hamlet*, with the emphasis upon the sword as a theatrical image, see the final section of chapter 4.

provides "satisfying reasons" for the murder of Cassio, while being placed behind a "bulk" (9, 1); when Cassio enters, Roderigo attacks. Moments later Othello enters to cheer on the murder in the dark. If Othello, observing Iago and Cassio in act 4, scene 1, stands in the same place on stage as does Roderigo awaiting Cassio in act 5, scene 1, a visual analogy could be established, while Othello's brief appearance in act 5, scene 1, could reinforce the equation if he is placed again in the same spot. Since throughout the play Roderigo has provided a constant image of folly and self-deception, to have Othello sink to such a level, even for a moment, could provide a telling effect. Similarly, in his final appearance in *Troilus and Cressida*, Hector—unarmed, admiring his newly won, sumptuous armor—could visually echo either Achilles sulking in his tent or Paris dallying with Helen (3. 1.). If so, Hector's final moments could link him visually to other flawed figures to whom his pursuit of questionable goals has brought him closer and closer.

Or consider the curious effect of the fourth scene of *Doctor Faustus*. At first glance Wagner's manipulation of Robin the clown seems to be a parody of the previous scene, with Wagner a debased version of Faustus and Robin a comic degradation of Mephostophilis. At the end of the scene, however, Robin (who has already taken the guilders to serve Wagner) has second thoughts and tries to back out of his bargain, at which point Wagner brings on two devils to enforce the pact. In the next scene Faustus makes his own bargain with Mephostophilis (asking for far more than a few guilders), but in scene 6 he too has second thoughts and calls on Christ to "help to save distressed Faustus' soul" (86). As in scene 4, this attempt to renege upon a bargain is squelched quickly, for Mephostophilis immediately returns with Lucifer and Beelzebub to frighten Faustus ("O, what art thou that look'st so terribly?—89). Like Robin, Faustus backs down quickly, asking for pardon, vowing "never to look to heaven, / Never to name God or to pray to him, / To burn his scriptures, slay his ministers, / And make my spirits pull his churches down" (98–101). Regardless of our initial impressions, Marlowe is presenting his tragic hero not as a Wagner figure of control but as a Robin who has made a bargain without realizing the full implications and who thereby is subject to the power of two devils (both here and in scene 19 when Lucifer and Beelzebub are again on stage, terrifying Faustus, driving his thoughts away from Christ's blood in the firmament). The appearances of two devils in scenes 4 and 6, if staged in parallel fashion, could heighten this ironic, deflationary analogue.

For an equivalent ironic effect one can turn to Shakespeare's presentation of Coriolanus's false assumptions about himself and Rome. Typically, Coriolanus responds to his banishment by the mob and the tribunes with "I banish you," adding, as he turns his back, "there is a world elsewhere" (3. 3. 123, 135). The disaffected hero here assumes that he can find a better world with Aufidius and the Volscians, free from the forces that have led to this disgrace. But in the latter part of the play Shakespeare demonstrates to the audience that the "world elsewhere" is no different from Rome. For example, at the beginning of act 3, scene 3, Sicinius and Brutus analyze their enemy's limitations, accurately predicting that, once angered, he will not be reined to temperance, for "then he speaks / What's in his heart, and that is there which looks / With us to break his neck" (28–30). Later, we again see and hear two figures, this time Aufidius and his lieutenant, analyzing Coriolanus's strengths and weaknesses, with Aufidius announcing that his fellow general "hath left undone / That which shall break his neck, or hazard mine, / When e'er we come to our account" (4. 7. 24–26). The verbal echo could be reinforced readily by parallel staging, especially if both scenes display two figures huddled together in conspiratorial fashion in a particular spot on stage. Or, again, when Coriolanus first seeks out Aufidius, the stage direction has him enter *"in mean apparel, disguis'd and muffled"* (4. 4. 0 s.d.); the overbearing hero then must endure a series of encounters with servants and commoners. This scene with the Volscians could provide a strong visual echo of act 2, scene 3, where Coriolanus, dressed in another kind of mean apparel (his gown of humility) had to come to terms with the Roman commoners who also were intimidated at first but later turned against him. Through these links Shakespeare undercuts his hero's assumptions about a world elsewhere by calling attention to continuity, not disparity, in his new career with Aufidius. Such analogies for the eye could heighten for the viewer the ironic force of the final acts.

In citing these analogues, my goal has been to establish the potential in this device through representative examples from well-known plays. Once aware of the possibilities, readers will be able to find equivalent, perhaps even better, examples elsewhere. Admittedly, there is no way to establish the authenticity of my suggested stagings, but what I have added to or inferred from the text (for example, the First Player's use of a sword) seems to me to follow from the logic of the play and to reinforce for the viewer what close readers have already discovered in the study. My concern, moreover, is not as much with the interpretations provided of *Hamlet* or *Edward II* as with the larger potential in the linking analogue for the critic, the director, and the historian.

Since my discussion so far has drawn largely upon the skills of the critic and the director, let me return in conclusion to the domain of the historian, at least to consider briefly the question: why should this device be especially suited to the drama in the age of Shakespeare? Granted, such analogues are to be found in any dramatic (or cinematic) medium where links for the eye can help to structure the experience of an audience, but this technique is not as apparent in Greek tragedy or Restoration comedy or even in much twentieth-century drama. Is there any historical reason why analogues for the eye are particularly appropriate to Elizabethan plays?

Several possible answers come to mind. First, the modern reader should mentally reconstruct the basic acting area for an Elizabethan company—a large, bare platform with no formal sets, no artificial lighting (except for the occasional torch), no extensive stage properties. Not only nature abhors a vacuum; critics and directors with reflexes conditioned by realism tend to *fill* this bare platform with personnel, properties, thrones, arbors, hangings—all the details necessary to satisfy *our* sense of "place." But let us, in our imaginations, leave this stage bare and then carefully, as in a controlled experiment, introduce one sword or one bishop or one poisoned kiss. On an unadorned, uncluttered stage, such a distinctive property or figure or action is not competing with many other details and is not absorbed into a rich, "busy" set. The viewer of such a production, it seems to me, would be more likely to perceive links between diverse dramatic moments because of less competition for his attention and greater emphasis upon the stage images that *are* provided. Although linking analogues certainly cannot be limited to the age of Shakespeare, with hindsight we can recognize how this device is particularly suited to the Elizabethan stage.

But the more difficult question remains: why were Elizabethan dramatists interested in such links in the first place? Here the historian must resort to generalizations about habits of mind or senses of structure peculiar to a given age. As noted in my first chapter, Joseph W. Donohue, Jr., has argued that in Fletcherian drama the intelligible unit is the scene, which often exists for its own sake; in such plays situations can be "deliberately brought out of the blue for the purpose of displaying human reactions to extreme and unexpected occurrences." In this kind of drama, links between divergent dramatic moments are of no particular help. But much medieval and Elizabethan art, as Madeleine Doran reminds us, is based upon a sense of "multiple unity" whereby many parts, often from different story lines, add up to some larger effect that draws upon an appreciation of "abundant variousness" or correspondences that prove meaningful. Although Fletcher's plays may lead us in a new direction, a habit of mind characteristic of the age of Shakespeare (and Sidney and Spenser) clearly supports the visual analogue.[8] Or, to use David Bevington's terms, in a drama that emphasizes coordination rather than subordination of one part to another, linking analogues could help the viewer "discover meaningful statement from a linear, episodic, and progressive sequence."

These tentative answers to a historical problem may seem far removed from the interests of modern readers and audiences. Yet the critic, working with links between characters or events in an Elizabethan play, can expect to find analogues to buttress his argument. The director faced with festival audiences will express little enthusiasm for the logic behind apparently excrescent moments (for example, the horseboy) and will prefer to streamline his acting text. But if we can assume that Shakespeare and his contemporaries did know their craft, we may discover a language for the eye woven into the fabric of such plays and thereby find meaning in moments that otherwise would appear peripheral or illogical. Modern audiences nurtured on the cinema need not be that far removed from a sense of patterned structure based upon visual repetition, a repetition that would be clearer on the open stage than on film. Here is a major example of how the pooling of the skills of historian, critic, and director can provide an extra dimension to this already impressive body of drama.

8. See my bibliography for a list of suggestive studies of analogous action and multiple unity in Elizabethan drama.

Chapter 4

Imagery and Symbolic Action for the Viewer's Eye

To turn from visual analogues to symbols and imagery is to move from relatively unknown terrain to a well-traveled highway. Much has been written from all possible points of view about imagery and symbolism in the plays of Shakespeare and his contemporaries—so much that to enter the lists again, for only one chapter, may seem an act worthy only of a Tamburlaine among critics. Certainly, the modern reader need not be reminded of the symbolic or imagistic (or emblematic or iconographic) potential in Elizabethan stage properties or costumes (or tableaux or gestures).[1] Yet even with this drawback of traversing again such familiar ground, there are still advantages in taking another look, from the perspective of the viewer's eye, at some revealing examples.

Let us start with some helpful comments on the Elizabethan stage and staging. After his careful analysis of the plays performed at the Globe between 1599 and 1609, Bernard Beckerman concludes that 80 percent of the scenes "need nothing but a bare

1. For some suggestive comments see Jocelyn Powell, "Marlowe's Spectacle," *Tulane Drama Review* 8 (1964): 195–210; Dieter Mehl, "Emblems in English Renaissance Drama," *Renaissance Drama* N.S. 2 (1969): 39–57; John Reibetanz, "Theatrical Emblems in *King Lear*," *Some Facets of "King Lear": Essays in Prismatic Criticism*, ed. Rosalie L. Colie and F. T. Flahiff (Toronto, 1974), pp. 39–57. For some important qualifications see Inga-Stina Ewbank, " 'More Pregnantly Than Words': Some Uses and Limitations of Visual Symbolism," *Shakespeare Survey* 24 (1971): 13–18.

space and an audience, not so much as a stool."[2] Our instinctive tendency, as heirs to a tradition of realism, to fill that stage with sets and properties therefore can be highly misleading. Pursuing this point, John Russell Brown notes that "the basic location of the play was the cleared space, in size some forty foot by thirty foot," and then argues: "Here the grouping of actors, the isolation of one or two, the costumes they wore, the hand-properties they carried (plays often demand sword, torch, prayer-book, bed, crown and so forth) and the gestures they used (wringing of hands, kneeling, kissing, running, 'making a stand' are often called for) were the dominant features of changing visual effects, given a focus by the frame and background of the unchanging platform." Brown concludes: "Always the appearance of the actor, his performance, his relation to others (and to empty space, doors or meaningful properties), are of prime importance, unsubdued and unemphasized by the elaborate scenery and expressive lighting effects that we are used to in modern theatres."[3] On such a stage details and actions stand out clearly, or, in Richard Southern's terms, moments on "the open stage" can be free "from the fetters of the trivial, the factual and the irrelevant, which exist in natural surroundings."[4]

The few properties or specified details that *are* introduced onto this uncluttered stage can be highly visible. Thus, on an elementary level, Elizabethan dramatists could use details or properties as a theatrical shorthand in place of elaborate exposition (or modern changes in scenery). To denote a change of scene to the country, a dramatist could direct: "*Enter* Strumbo *with a pitchfork*" (*Locrine*); to suggest that his characters have just arrived after a journey, he might direct: "*Enter* Sir Bartram *with* Eustace *and others, booted*" (*James IV*) or "*Enter* Lacy, Warren, Ermsby, *booted and spurred*" (*Friar Bacon and Friar Bungay*); to

2. *Shakespeare at the Globe 1599–1609* (New York, 1962), p. 106.
3. *Shakespeare's Dramatic Style* (New York, 1972), p. 12.
4. *The Open Stage* (London, 1953), p. 73.

place his action in a tavern, *"enter* Verone *with his napkin upon his shoulder, . . . and his son bringing in cloth and napkins"* (*An Humourous Day's Mirth*); to denote a recently concluded meal off-stage: *"Enter hastily at several doors:* Duke of Lancaster, Duke of York, *the* Earls of Arundel *and* Surrey, *with napkins on their arms and knives in their hands"* (*Woodstock*) or *"enter* Frankford, *as it were brushing the crumbs from his clothes with a napkin, as newly risen from supper"* (*A Woman Killed with Kindness*). Such shorthand was undoubtedly a common practice, perhaps too common to require specific authorial directions in every instance. We should keep in mind the appeal made by the Chorus at the outset of *Henry V* that the viewer "piece out our imperfections with your thoughts," thereby using his imaginary forces to supply the tavern or dinner or journey that cannot be represented physically on the open stage.

Such examples of dramatic shorthand may seem elementary to the modern reader, but they represent a first step toward equally obvious but more significant use of theatrical details. As a second step, let me turn to a revealing example of a symbolic costume (and stage property) where for a change the historian can provide some external evidence. In his suggestive study of the principles behind Elizabethan stage costume, Hal H. Smith argues that the limited funds available would have been spent where they would yield the most benefits in dramatic terms—costumes for major characters. He then notes that in 1600 the tight-fisted Henslowe gave his company a pound "to buy a gray gown for Grissil"; as Smith goes on to argue, this unprepossessing costume takes on considerable importance in Dekker's play (*Patient Grissill*), charting the heroine's "changing social position" and drawing attention to a major theme, "the contrast between opulent vice and virtuous poverty."[5] A closer look at

5. "Some Principles of Elizabethan Stage Costume," *Journal of the Warburg and Courtauld Institutes* 25 (1962): 243. See R. A. Foakes and R. T. Rickert, eds., *Henslowe's Diary* (Cambridge, 1961), p. 130.

the play, in fact, can tell us even more. Early in the comedy Grissill's father stresses their poverty by noting that her portion from him "is but an honest name" while "thy silks are thread-bare russets" (1. 2. 48–49). When Marquess Gwalter begins to test his new wife in act 2, he observes sarcastically that the monuments of her "nobility" (her gown, hat, and pitcher) are hanging on the wall to stress her origins; Grissill responds meekly that she is ready to cast off her courtly garb ("all this outside") and wear again "this russet bravery of my own" (2. 2. 63–76). In act 3 the gown and pitcher are still hanging on stage among Gwalter's costliest gems ("see here they hang") when he again confronts his wife with her supposed pride, claiming "you have forgot these rags, this water pot" (3. 1. 80–89). Subsequently, when he sends Grissill home, the marquess tells his men to "disrobe her of these rich habiliments, / Take down her hat, her pitcher, and her gown, / And as she came to me in beggary, / So drive her to her father's" (4. 1. 170–73); moments later Grissill herself gives further symbolic value to the gown and pitcher, pointing out that both are unworn and unhurt after her years at court (4. 2. 74–87). In a simple yet forceful way this costume and property provide a highly visible symbolic constant by which the audience can measure both Grissill, who is not affected by the trappings of the court, and the sycophants, Mario and Lepido, who accept at face value Gwalter's strictures. Much of Dekker's thesis and demonstration is linked to this one costume which was important enough to warrant a special investment by Henslowe.

The reader may question the value of this example from such a limited, obvious play. The historian will find no new principle here; the director certainly needs no reminding of the potential value in costume; the critic is already aware of the importance of symbolic clothing in a wide range of Elizabethan plays (*Woodstock*, *King Lear*, *The Tempest*). But the modern reader can easily forget how *obvious* such an effect can be, especially on the open stage with no pretensions to realism. When dealing with Grissill's gown and pitcher, the critic or director is not working with a motif deeply embedded in the text that requires careful extraction, but rather is rediscovering an effect that a viewer watching the original production probably would not have missed. I am not arguing that the less obvious symbolic meanings found by the critic in Elizabethan actions or properties or tableaux are suspect or inferior. Rather, I am suggesting that our twentieth-century desire for subtlety and realism can at times screen out basic, obvious effects that would have been (and still could be) highly visible to the viewer's eye.

Consider the following scene from one of the non-Shakespearean plays most praised for its "realism," Heywood's *A Woman Killed with Kindness*.[6] When the justly indignant Frankford pursues his wife's seducer across the stage, the stage direction reads: *"Enter* Wendoll, *running over the stage in a night gown, he after him with his sword drawn; the Maid in her smock stays his hand and clasps hold on him. He pauses awhile"* (scene 13, line 67 s.d.). After his pause, Frankford states: "I thank thee, maid; thou like the angel's hand / Hast stay'd me from a bloody sacrifice" (68–69). The critic or director working with realistic assumptions may indeed wonder why the Maid, who is anything but a developed "character" in this play, is on stage at all, much less a major force in the action. But, at least for this dramatic moment, Heywood has little concern for realism in our sense. Rather the reference to "the angel's hand" gives a clear symbolic value to this supernumerary figure; the drawn sword, associated with revenge and anger and justice, is here "stayed" by another force (mercy/reason) associated with a power greater than man, an intervention that sets up Frankford's pivotal decision to leave Wendoll to his guilty conscience and to kill his wife with kindness. The combination of the two figures (Frankford,

6. Text used is the Revels edition, ed. R. W. Van Fossen (London, 1961).

the Maid), the key property (the sword), and the action or inter-action (staying the sword, then the pause) produce a striking theatrical effect that calls attention to a decision at the heart of the play. The lack of "realism" here need not be a liability; rather, the appearance of the Maid and Frankford's reaction create a special emphasis, a theatrical *italics*, that singles out such a moment for the eye (and mind) of the viewer.

The dramatist need not resort to a supernumerary Maid or an obviously symbolic pitcher and gray gown to gain such an effect. Take, for example, the practical joke that Prince Hal plays upon Francis the drawer in *1 Henry IV*. Critics usually argue that the prince's testing of the drawer's bond to the vintner is Hal's way of expressing his own awareness of bonds, debts, and tru-ancy. Usually overlooked, however, is the obvious and striking stage business. Thus, the prince on one side keeps drawing Fran-cis back to him by offering various rewards, while Poins, offstage, uses the drawer's name to elicit a mechanistic response (verbally —"Anon, sir"; physically—a movement toward the speaker), a response that eventually causes Hal to conclude: "That ever this fellow should have fewer words than a parrot, and yet the son of a woman!" (2. 4. 98–99). Interestingly, Poins never grasps the purpose of the action; he asks Hal: "But hark ye, what cunning match have you made with this jest of the drawer? Come, what's the issue?" (89–91). Rather it is the audience that sees a minor figure act out his limitations, jerked back and forth like a puppet on two strings until: "*Here they both call him; the drawer stands amazed, not knowing which way to go*" (79 s.d.). Francis's stage movement could set up a visual analogue with Hotspur's behavior, either during his wife's long speech in the previous scene or during act 1, scene 3, when he too had been manipu-lated by two figures, Worcester and Northumberland. Whether we recognize such a specific link, the drawer's frenetic, puppet-like behavior sets up for the viewer a lively demonstration of a figure controlled by others, unable to cope with the strings that manipulate him, while establishing the prince as a controller or puppetmaster rather than one of those controlled. The more extreme and unrealistic the staging, the more effective would be the symbolic point. To present the scene in a restrained, subdued fashion might satisfy our sense of realism or propriety, especially if we are concerned about Hal's heartlessness or bad taste, but such a choice by critic or director easily could undermine or obscure the larger point for the viewer's eye. Or, in other terms, for this moment symbolic action may take precedence over "character."

Such striking stage movements or stage relationships with obvious symbolic meanings are not unusual in Elizabethan plays. Similar contrasts between controlled and controlling figures can be found in *The Jew of Malta*, where Barabas appears above, almost as a presiding deity, to overlook the duel he has caused between Mathias and Lodowick that leads to both their deaths (3. 2.), or in *The Tempest*, where the audience is conscious of the benign presence of Prospero in the background during the love duet between Ferdinand and Miranda (3. 1.) and above, invisible to those below, during the banquet for the courtiers (3. 3.). An even more emphatic contrast between the controller and the controlled or the victor and the vanquished occurs in some well-known scenes in which an erect figure stands over a prostrate opponent with more than physical victory at stake: Prince Hal standing over both Hotspur and Falstaff (and perhaps also the body of Sir Walter Blunt disguised as Henry IV); Iago standing over Othello, crooning "work on, my medicine, work" (4. 1.); Volpone standing over Voltore during the sham dispossession (5. 12.), acting out his power over the advocate by voiding him not of a devil but of his conscience. In the latter instance, moreover, Voltore is not an inert, lifeless figure but rather a writhing, contorted shammer (Volpone gives him such instructions as "stop your wind hard, and swell") whose obvious descent from the impressive, successful advocate of act 4 acts out Jonson's point about obsession and the power of gold. Similarly, other special physical relationships can be rendered with theatrical italics. Quite striking are the scenes in which one figure carries another: Falstaff bearing off Hotspur's body (perhaps recalling the Devil in the moralities bearing off the Vice or Worldly Man); Orlando bringing in old Adam on his back (thereby giving the lie to the value judgment on the seventh age of man provided by Jaques); Humphrey Wasp in *Bartholomew Fair* getting Bartholomew Cokes on his back (only to find that he has assumed his "charge" or "burden" too late). Undoubtedly, the reader can provide his own list of such meaningful moments: kneelings, embraces, joined hands.

My intention, however, is to focus upon unusual or unexpected moments because the more striking the action (and the less in keeping with modern assumptions), the more it cries out for symbolic interpretation. Thus, in a curious group of scenes apparently dead figures rise to confront the audience. In *The Jew of Malta*, Ferneze and the Maltese Christians throw the seemingly dead body of Barabas over the walls, thinking that they have rid themselves of the Jew (5. 1.), but the wily Barabas rises to tell the audience that he will be revenged upon Malta, and he immediately helps the invading Turks to enter the town. What Barabas represents or has come to represent cannot be readily purged from Malta; here, as elsewhere in this sardonic play, Marlowe undermines the pat assumptions of the ruling Christians about the heavens and their own inherent superiority to Jew and Turk. The most famous figure to rise from the dead in this manner is, of course, Falstaff at the end of *1 Henry IV* whose rise and speech on counterfeiting demonstrate that he, like Barabas, embodies something that cannot be destroyed easily (perhaps prefiguring Hal's backsliding in the sequel). When Falstaff wounds and then bears off the body of Hotspur, he gains an honor that may be a lie or counterfeit, but nonetheless is associated with life and worldly success (as opposed to the grinning honor of Sir Walter Blunt or the brittle honor of Hot-spur). A different but related effect is achieved in *The Malcontent* where the villainous Mendoza thinks he is poisoning his sup-posed accomplice, Malevole, with an empty box. But with the departure of Mendoza, Malevole (really the virtuous Duke Alto-front in disguise) rises from apparent death, shedding his mal-content disguise and setting in motion the final reversal that will oust the villain and reclaim the throne for the rightful duke. The symbolic death of the villainous, foul-mouthed Malevole (a role forced upon the formerly naïve, impolitic duke) thus coincides with the final movement of the play that leads to the eventual ordering. "Malevole" may be dead, but Altofront clearly has survived and learned the necessary lessons (that "mature dis-cretion is the life of state"—4. 5. 146). In what may be a reminis-cence of Marston's scene, the author of *The Revenger's Tragedy* has his protagonist, Vindice, dress the dead body of the mur-dered duke in the garments of "Piato," the disguise worn by Vindice for much of the play while in the service of Lussurioso. No figure here rises from the dead, but Vindice in a sense attacks and murders his former identity. Moreover, the visual equation between the duke (the hated enemy) and Piato (a role taken on by the revenger) suggests a growing similarity between villain and supposed hero (an effect also enhanced by the linking analogues cited in chapter 3). In all these moments, striking and provocative stage actions that defy our realistic expectations call attention to symbolic life or set up equations in a way calculated to surprise or shock a viewer into heightened awareness of the issues at stake.

There are many other obvious, emphatic ways to convey symbolic meanings for the viewer's eye. Readers undoubtedly are familiar with Richard II's symbolic descent to the base court of Bolingbroke at Flint Castle or Antony's descent in the forum scene to the physical and symbolic level of the plebeians; in contrast, Tamburlaine mounts to his chair in act 4, scene 2, of part 1 by using the stooping Bajazeth as his footstool, while Barabas literally and figuratively falls into a trap of his own devising at the end of *The Jew of Malta*. Or again, as critics have noted, striking effects can be gained by the breaking of some symbolic object: Friar Bacon breaking his magic glass; the shrewish Kate breaking her sister's lute; Richard II breaking his mirror in the deposition scene; Hamlet breaking the recorder. The association of the lute with harmony or the mirror with self-awareness (or vanity or both) can be conveyed vividly through such a charged moment. Stage business involving crowns (such as Richard II and Bolingbroke in the deposition scene or Tamburlaine and Mycetes) can be obvious as can stage business with thrones or armor or other potentially charged objects highly visible on the open stage. The more detailed the parody of religion, the more striking would be the effect of Volpone's morning hymn to his gold that opens the play; the more striking the contrast between Bajazeth in his cage and Tamburlaine with his feast of crowns in act 4, scene 4, the more meaningful the contrast between the losers bound fast in their iron chains of subjection and the victor inexorably challenging fate and conventional morality. Bizarre, unrealistic effects fit well with the open stage and the viewer's eye.

To ignore or play down such moments so as not to offend realistic expectations is to pass over possibilities that may be central to their respective plays. Consider, as a particularly striking example, Kyd's use of an empty box and the death of a minor villain in *The Spanish Tragedy*.[7] To dispose of unreliable accomplices, the arch-villain Lorenzo, who trusts only himself (3. 2. 118), convinces his servant, Pedringano, to murder Serberine; Pedringano, who foolishly trusts his master (3. 3. 13–14), is arrested soon after the murder by the watchmen who had been told to guard closely that spot. Once captured, Pedringano is persuaded not to confess his various crimes by the promise from Lorenzo

7. Text used is the Revels edition, ed. Philip Edwards (London, 1959).

of a pardon, which is supposedly being conveyed in a box by a page. But in act 3, scene 5, the boy, alone on stage, peeks in the box and spells out the situation for the audience:

> By my bare honesty, here's nothing but the bare empty box: were it not sin against secrecy, I would say it were a piece of gentlemanlike knavery. I must go to Pedringano, and tell him his pardon is in this box, nay, I would have sworn it, had I not seen the contrary. I cannot choose but smile to think how the villain will flout the gallows, scorn the audience, and descant on the hangman, and all presuming of his pardon from hence. Will 't not be an odd jest, for me to stand and grace every jest he makes, pointing my finger at this box, as who would say, "Mock on, here's thy warrant." Is't not a scurvy jest, that a man should jest himself to death?
>
> [6–17]

I quote this passage at length because it sets up the necessary stage business for the execution scene that follows. Here Pedringano asks the hangman if the latter sees "yonder boy with the box in his hand?" with the response, "What, he that points to it with his finger?" (65–66). Pedringano then asks: "What hath he in his box, as thou think'st?" (73) and, in response to the hangman's comment about his soul's health, observes "that that is good for the body is likewise good for the soul: and it may be, in that box is balm for both" (76–78). Thus, throughout the scene, the condemned man jokes with the hangman and with Hieronimo (who comments that "I have not seen a wretch so impudent!"—89), exhibiting literal and figurative gallows humor and pointing with naïve confidence to the boy and the box, while the page too points and grins in the same broad, obvious fashion. Admittedly, for the reader this sardonic demise of a minor villain is easily overshadowed by Hieronimo's growing anguish, which is well orchestrated in this scene, but, if staged with appropriate force, Kyd's carefully wrought presentation could add an obvious symbolic dimension to the entire play. For if this scene sets up in dramatic italics Pedringano's misplaced trust in an empty box, the viewer readily can make the leap to the range of figures in this tragedy (Horatio, Bel-Imperia, Hieronimo, even Lorenzo) who fail or falter because of an equivalent misplaced trust (in Fortune, in the safety of a trysting place, in the fidelity of others); in fact, each of the figures who is destroyed or destroys himself has his own distinctive version of the empty box, even going blithely to his end (as in the play-within-the-play of act 4) with Pedringano's combination of blindness and confidence. Indeed, Don Andrea himself, who little knows at the outset how many deaths his revenge eventually will entail, may be the ultimate truster in the empty box. This bizarre execution scene, then, can be a fine demonstration of the richness of a symbolic action on the open stage.

In singling out examples of obvious symbolic action on the open stage, I have not drawn upon Shakespeare's major tragedies. The reader familiar with a play like *King Lear* can supply his own list of equivalent moments: the dividing of the crown in the opening scene; the fool giving his coxcomb to Kent (1. 4.); Kent in the stocks juxtaposed with Oswald rewarded and Edgar reduced to nothing (2. 2. through 2. 4.); Goneril and Regan joining hands in front of a shocked Lear (2. 4.); the appearance of Poor Tom and Lear's question: "Is man no more than this?" (3. 4.); and more. Although the impact of such moments *is* striking and obvious, the complex web of themes and relationships in such a tragedy does not lend itself readily to the summary treatment used in the preceding pages. To do even limited justice to symbolic action (or imagistic patterns) in the major tragedies requires considerably more space than is feasible here. Two such moments from *Othello* and *King Lear* will, therefore, be treated in the next chapter under a special heading, while an extended discussion of Hamlet's sword will conclude this chapter.

My reluctance to plunge into Shakespeare's major tragedies is based upon the conviction that, before taking on the subtleties and complexities of symbolic action in *King Lear* and *Hamlet*, the modern reader first should learn to recognize and appreciate the obvious in principle and action. For complex cultural and psychological reasons (which I do not claim to understand), the modern demand is consistently for subtlety in literary interpretation and effect, to the point where the obvious, so long ignored or scorned, can itself become elusive or subtle. But the Elizabethans apparently could present and welcome obvious, highly visible, symbolic actions (whether Grissill's gown or a puppet-like Francis or figures rising from the dead or Pedringano's empty box), thereby relieving the critic or director of the responsibility of generating his own set of symbols. My emphasis, moreover, has been primarily upon symbolic *actions* wherein figures or objects move or interact before the viewer's eye to gain that added visibility produced by motion or stage life. Ironically, belaboring the obvious can be a fruitful way of calling attention to a subtlety and complexity in Elizabethan drama that have been lost for many readers but could have been highly visible to the original audience.

Such strictures about the obvious need not, of course, apply only to symbolic action. As suggested, for example, by Kyd's presentation of the empty box, some highly visible moments do not stand alone but rather grow out of or relate to other themes, motifs, and actions in their plays. When treating such possibilities, especially in the plays of Shakespeare, the critic is again on familiar ground, finding further expression of iterative patterns woven throughout the fabric of the plays or, to use the most familiar term, further examples of imagery. For decades, careful readers of Shakespeare have demonstrated the value of isolating and discussing these patterns; imagistic criticism in its many varieties remains one of the most popular and fruitful approaches to Elizabethan drama.

But, unfortunately, many readers still conceive of imagery solely in verbal or poetic terms, even though there have been repeated calls for an expanded conception of stage imagery or presentational imagery or dramatic metaphor that would go beyond the strictly verbal limits of the text. A forceful spokesman for this latter position, Maurice Charney, has argued: "The words are, after all, only a part of the full imaginative experience of the play, and, especially for a writer so thoroughly immersed in the theater as Shakespeare, there are many nonverbal elements in a performance which work together with the poetry of the text and help to express it. We may say, then, that the play an audience sees creates its own set of images and metaphors that are not merely those of the spoken lines." Charney's concern, then, is with that "large body of images that is not part of the spoken words of the text, but directly presented in the theater," for here is where "the drama moves outside the reaches of a strictly verbal art" in its use of another language, one "of gesture and stage properties," which can communicate meanings to an audience.[8]

Several corollaries follow from Charney's position. Consider first the importance of the sequence or progression of an Elizabethan play—its flow of language, events, and staging in time. As Charney points out, a play in the theater is "a continuous temporal unit"; in other terms, "we cannot go back to pick up something we missed."[9] As a result, behind any study of repetitive patterns (of language, of imagery) in a play in the theater lurks the question: what is perceived at what moment by whom? Granted, many devoted readers have committed major portions of *Hamlet* to the book and volume of their brains; nonetheless, a viewer in the theater experiencing that play for the first time (or even the second or third) would lack the total control over the text demanded (or implied) in many imagistic studies. Spenser

8. *Shakespeare's Roman Plays: The Function of Imagery in the Drama* (Cambridge, Mass., 1961), pp. 4–5, 7–9. See also the studies listed in my bibliography under "Imagery for the Viewer's Eye."
9. Ibid., p. 10.

told his prospective bride that "none can call again the passed time"; similarly, no viewer can call again the passed moment of a play on stage. Although the reader easily can flip back a page in his annotated text, such a flip during a performance requires a remarkable memory. Thus the patterns created on the page by careful, sensitive readers sometimes assume a total unity never present in the theater, even for an attentive and sophisticated audience. Behind such patterns occasionally lurk questionable assumptions about the human memory, not to mention the degree of awareness expected of the listener. Thus, the author of a recent and perceptive study of figurative patterns in *Hamlet* could argue that a description in act 2 "recalls" an action in act 3 or that "the accounts of the Ghost's early appearances contain reminders of a form and a formula of the dumb show."[10] To such a critic, all words and events are present simultaneously; drama has ceased to be an event in time with a sequence, a progression, an accretion of meaning as the play unfolds. But if the critic is to be faithful to the play as play in its native habitat, he must take into account the time continuum in which that play exists and the sequence of images under consideration. To ignore the temporal movement of the play—in extreme form, to assume knowledge of act 5 in act 1—is to falsify the experience of the audience and to pervert the dramatic logic basic to much Elizabethan theater.

To pursue a related issue, not infrequently a critic will point to a pattern of imagery in a major Shakespearean play which purportedly has gone unnoticed. But if such an image cluster

10. Lee Sheridan Cox, *Figurative Design in "Hamlet,"*: *The Significance of the Dumb Show* (Columbus, Ohio, 1973), pp. 19–20. Clifford Lyons has aptly termed this approach the "radar" method in which "the play is scanned back and forth, and back, each detail minutely reëxamined in the light of every other detail, from end to beginning," a process, he argues, that "derogates a dramaturgy which tells a story for maximum theatrical effects in a skillfully arranged sequence of scenes." See his "Shakespeare's Plays: 'devis'd and play'd to take spectators'—Some Critical Implications," *Renaissance Papers 1968*, ed. George Walton Williams (The Southeastern Renaissance Conference, 1969), p. 62.

has eluded careful readers for almost four centuries, can it be expected to elicit a response even from a trained and alert audience? In short, is such an image operative? This yardstick will appear irrelevant to that critic poring over *Hamlet* as a dramatic poem, but should be weighed carefully by any reader contemplating that tragedy as a play on stage in performance. My purpose is not to deny poetic subtlety in Shakespeare or Elizabethan drama; the existence of complex iterative patterns in these plays has been amply demonstrated. Rather, I am trying to use the skills of both the historian and the director to call attention to critical interpretations that have little chance of being realized for an audience. Shakespeare, after all, was a professional man of the theater who knew his medium well. He certainly did not shy away from repetition when he wished to establish a theme or image for his listeners. In the opening scene of *King Lear* the word "nothing" is repeated five times within a few lines, while the emphasis upon "name" is patently obvious during the balcony scene of *Romeo and Juliet*. For a major image to be operative in a play (or any oral-aural medium), some such introduction is necessary so that the development of the pattern —the accretion of meaning—will be recognized by an audience that lacks concordances and computers, an audience that must depend upon its ears, in fact upon one hearing of a given speech. As noted earlier in discussing symbolic action, to be fair to the achievement of Elizabethan plays we cannot ignore the obvious in favor of a modern penchant for subtlety and indirection.

Kenneth Burke, in his analysis of symbolic action in literature, provides another criterion for evaluating imagistic patterns. The most obvious method of determining the importance of an image, he observes, is the quantitative approach (as typified by the work of Caroline Spurgeon)—how many times does that image occur in the text? But Burke asks: "Might there not also be the *qualitative* importance of beginning, middle, and end? That is: should we not attach particular significance to the situations on which the work opens and closes, and the events by which the peripety, or reversal is contrived?"—what Burke terms "the laying of the cornerstone," the "watershed moment," and the "valedictory" or "funeral wreath."[11] According to this formulation, a truly important image or motif should be orchestrated and indeed emphasized at crucial or pivotal moments.

Although Burke's criterion is derived from a discussion of *The Ancient Mariner*, his concern with the qualitative importance of imagery certainly is applicable to the drama, especially since the dramatist is not limited solely to verbal display of a major image at climactic points in the action but can resort as well to stage business, costumes, groupings, sound effects, and other nonverbal devices to underscore a developing pattern for the viewer. Thus, in the orchard scene Brutus places heavy verbal emphasis upon blood, seeing the conspirators as sacrificers rather than murderers, carvers rather than butchers, yet this blood imagery is not fully developed until after the assassination (certainly a watershed moment) when the conspirators in full view of the audience bathe their hands in Caesar's blood and engage in the bloody shaking of hands with Antony, a series of bloody actions clearly linked to the major themes of the play. Or, for an often-cited example, the verbal emphasis upon sleep and sleeplessness in *Macbeth* is embodied visually and theatrically in the justly famous sleepwalking scene near the climax of that tragedy. In both instances (and more could be cited), a major image that already has received careful verbal development has been expressed forcefully through an action or a visual effect, through enactment rather than mere description. Such effects can be particularly striking when the careful poetic preparation builds to as noteworthy a scene as Lady Macbeth's sleepwalking or Giovanni's entrance in *'Tis Pity She's a Whore* with Annabella's

11. *The Philosophy of Literary Form: Studies in Symbolic Action*, revised edition (New York, 1957), pp. 59–60. Burke later observes (p. 66): "We should watch for 'critical points' within the work, as well as at beginnings and endings. There are often 'watershed moments,' changes of slope, where some new quality enters."

heart on his dagger. The effect of such moments has much to do with the sequence and progression of the imagistic pattern.

The critic interested in iterative patterns in the plays of Shakespeare and his contemporaries should be conscious of both the rich poetic texture *and* other sources of imagery. To do so is often to find further support for the claims of careful readers or, as suggested earlier, to discover ways of making subtle points quite obvious for the viewer's eye. For example, readers of *Coriolanus* have noted the protagonist's fierce desire for independence and self-sufficiency, his striving to act "as if a man were author of himself, / And knew no other kin" (5. 3. 36–37). A great deal of textual support can be adduced for this "man alone" theme, but equally important is the long series of scenes in which Coriolanus is on stage with either a mob or other distinctive, cohesive groups (senators, family). The themes of the tragedy are enhanced if the viewer is continually aware of the tragic hero, as isolated individual, facing and separated from other groups or factions which ideally should be linked to the strong right arm of the body politic (especially if figures like Menenius, Aufidius, and the tribunes are not isolated in this fashion). Such staging possibilities have as much claim to imagistic analysis as the rich and complex language that points us in the same direction. As with Kyd's empty box or Shakespeare's puppetlike Francis, moments presented with theatrical italics can be almost invisible to the reader only conscious of the words.

In order to substantiate these claims, let me offer two more extensive examples. The first comes from a play not known for its imagery or iterative patterns, the anonymous *Woodstock*,[12] and consists of an unusual motif for such development—whispering. After Richard II has rejected his uncles in favor of his fawning advisers, he reappears with new attire, with a guard of

12. Text used is *Woodstock: A Moral History*, ed. A. P. Rossiter (London, 1946).

archers, and also with a new bit of obvious stage business. Thus the king enters with his favorites (Bushy, Bagot, Greene, and Scroope) and with "Tresilian, *whispering with the* King" (3. 1. 0 s.d.). This whispering is linked immediately to Tresilian's plan for the blank charters and the abuse of the kingdom; moreover, such real abuses are soon contrasted to the hapless situation of the English people, for later in this scene Tresilian (probably whispering again) tells Nimble "to mark who grudges, or but speaks amiss / Of good King Richard . . . myself . . . or any of his new councillors. / Attach them all for privy whisperers / And send them up" (131–34). In obvious contrast, Woodstock, Lancaster, and York hear of the blank charters in the next scene, undoubtedly shouting and exclaiming (see lines 67–78); later, Woodstock refuses to go to court, arguing that his "English plainness will not suit that place" (228), again distinguishing himself from the whisperers.

Subsequent scenes then distinguish clearly between real and supposed whisperers. First, Nimble again is charged to "look to the whisperers" (3. 3. 35), so he and Bailey Ignorance stand on one part of the stage (probably whispering their lines) in order to overhear and arrest a series of figures who speak against Tresilian and the blank charters. The butcher, the grazier, and the farmer (who speaks of "whispering knaves abroad"— 85–86) are marked as whisperers (56–57), as is the whistler (223), while Fleming later reports of "seven hundred sent up to th' court for whisperers" (268–69). Tresilian's appearance *"with bags of money"* (4. 1. 0 s.d.) shows how the whisperers at court are profiting, while further references to the seven hundred whisperers (4. 3. 8–9, 71) and the arrest of the shrieves of Kent and Northumberland for defending their ancient liberties demonstrate the fate of those who speak out and tell the truth. The links among the various instances of insidious whispering could be quite obvious for the viewer's eye if such moments (Richard II with Tresilian, Tresilian with Nimble, Nimble with Ignorance) are staged in analogous fashion—for example, if each time the two figures huddle together in the same spot on stage. Another possible link in the chain is provided by Richard's entrance with Greene, with Bushy providing the comment: "See, see! he comes; and that flattering hound Greene close at's elbow" (4. 1. 64–65). Greene's influence, we soon find out, is crucial in persuading the king to farm out his kingdom to four favorites (138–62), a second startling abuse which could be associated with courtly whispering.

The third and, in dramatic terms, most significant abuse associated with whispering then follows with the capture and eventual death of Woodstock, the most outspoken figure in the play, the man most opposed to courtly whispering. Woodstock's undoing starts with a considerable amount of noise: "*A flourish of cornets. Then a great shout and winding of horns*" (4. 2. 101 s.d.); Cynthia's speech and the masque are followed by the typical comments of Plain Thomas on the king, his flatterers, and the state of England. But when news comes that the house is beset with armed men, Woodstock turns to the masquers: "Hear me, gentlemen . . . / (Fore God I do not like this whispering) / If your intents be honest, show your faces" (163–65). On orders of the king (who refuses to shed his disguise or admit his presence), Woodstock's mouth finally is stopped even though this outspoken figure defends himself verbally (as do the shrieves in the next scene) and recognizes the fate in store for him. The motif might be orchestrated once again in act 5 where LaPoole and the two murderers could also be staged as whisperers; regardless, in this pivotal scene in act 4 the insidious courtly whisperers have defeated and destroyed the plain speaker of truth. As York says later of his brother, "It was an easy task to work on him, / His plainness was too open to their view: / He feared no wrong, because his heart was true" (5. 3. 6–8).

Here then we have an iterative pattern which can clarify and develop issues basic to this play. On the one hand, the dramatist presents the concocted crime of privy whispering as a device for making money or abusing law and tradition, yet the victims of such abuses often are admirable, outspoken, and fearless (the shrieves, Woodstock). The actual whispering, obvious to the viewer's eye, is performed by the men who manipulate the king, betray Woodstock, and rape the country in the panoramic act 3, scene 3. With his blunt honesty and plain speaking, Woodstock embodies the alternative to such whispering and perhaps is destroyed for that reason. Given appropriate staging, the effect could be obvious and striking and could establish important distinctions for the audience in the theater.

To move from *Woodstock* to *Hamlet* is, in imagistic terms, to move from an untapped vein to the mother lode. Indeed, to contribute another imagistic gloss to the margins of this tragedy would seem to provide prima facie evidence of either critical hubris or an antic disposition. My focus—Hamlet's sword—may seem less than central, moreover, to the reader already saturated with the many patterns and possibilities offered by this much-discussed play. My choice of weapons, however, is deliberate (there is no sense in my "being remiss, / Most generous, and free from all contriving"), for few readers will have considered this particular iterative image as a unifying device or even as a recurring symbol of any significance. Yet therein lies my point. The usual *reading* of this tragedy concerned largely with verbal effects will not establish the sword as a crucial element either poetically or structurally. Although weapons continually may be called to our attention (who knows not "bare bodkin"?), there is no famous speech, no purple passage, to make Hamlet's sword part of our cultural arsenal. But regardless of any lack of emphasis for the reader, Hamlet's sword does play a highly significant role for any viewer of the play and for that reader conscious of presentational as well as verbal effects. An analysis of the sequence of scenes in which swords play a decisive role thereby can show how the accretion of meaning associated with this theatrical image can lead an audience into a greater understanding of a major theme of the tragedy.

Hamlet's sword is first called to our attention during act 1, scenes 4 and 5, the first meeting between hero and ghost. The first parapet scene had stressed the Danish preparations for war and had introduced the armed ghost with his "martial stalk" (1. 1. 66). Upon hearing of this visitation, Hamlet had mused upon "my father's spirit—in arms!" and had concluded: "All is not well" (1. 2. 254). Now in act 1, scene 4, Hamlet meets this armed ghost and at some point during the scene draws his sword. Admittedly, there are no helpful stage directions and no verbal references to swords in general or to Hamlet's sword in particular, but the warning delivered to Horatio and Marcellus ("Unhand me, gentlemen. / By heaven, I'll make a ghost of him that lets me!"—84–85) makes far better dramatic sense if spoken with drawn sword in hand (and apparently always has been acted that way). According to stage tradition, when Hamlet follows the ghost offstage he already has his sword unsheathed, whether he is pointing it at the ghost (Garrick) or trailing it behind him (Kemble) or using the hilt as a cross to be held in front of him (Booth).[13] The latter staging (widely used in modern productions) would follow logically from Hamlet's first speech to the ghost, for the sword-cross in his hands becomes an apparent source of Christian value ("angels and ministers of grace defend us!"—39), a weapon against goblins damned or "blasts from hell."

The subsequent interview with the ghost includes no mention of swords, although the intense passage of ninety lines builds to an exhortation to revenge, an act later to be associated with that weapon. But in the problematic cellarage scene that concludes act 1, scene 5, Hamlet's sword becomes the obvious

13. See Arthur Colby Sprague, *Shakespeare and the Actors* (Cambridge, Mass., 1944), pp. 140–41.

verbal and visual focus both for those on stage and for the audience. Within fifteen lines "swear by my sword" or "upon my sword" is repeated six times along with the gestures and stage business necessary for three such oaths. Clearly this weapon is being called to our attention in that emphatic manner Shakespeare normally reserves for only his major images or themes.

Unfortunately, critics do not agree on how to interpret the cellarage scene, one of the many puzzling moments in this puzzling play.[14] One reason for the confusion and the debate may be our tendency to focus primarily upon the ghost rather than upon the obvious and striking stage business. Even though the eerie presence beneath the stage does cast its shadow upon the dramatic action, the eyes and immediate attention of the audience are drawn not to that unseen supernatural figure but rather to Hamlet's sword which serves as a focal point, a magnet that three times draws together the figures on stage and even the voice below. In fact, many facets of this scene become more meaningful when the dramatic emphasis is placed upon the sword rather than upon the ghost or Hamlet's antic behavior. If Booth's staging of Hamlet's exit in act 1, scene 4, is accepted, the use of the sword here as a quasi-holy object upon which an oath can be sworn would come as no surprise.[15] But the initial effect of the father's spirit upon his son in act 1, scene 4, we should remember, was to turn that same sword against two friends and allies. On the one hand, the emphatic presence of Hamlet's

14. For one standard interpretation (that "father and son seem to be playing into each other's hands in order to hoodwink an inconvenient witness," Marcellus) see John Dover Wilson, *What Happens in "Hamlet"*, third edition (Cambridge, 1951), pp. 80–83; for a critique of Wilson's answer, along with the alternative argument that Shakespeare is stressing the diabolic origins of the ghost, see Eleanor Prosser, *Hamlet and Revenge* (Stanford, 1967), pp. 140–41.

15. Such stage use of a sword for oaths was by no means uncommon. In *The Spanish Tragedy* (often linked to *Hamlet*), Lorenzo enjoins Pedringano to "swear on this cross [that is, the hilt of the sword], that what thou say'st is true" and concludes: "But if I prove thee perjur'd and unjust, / This very sword whereon thou took'st thine oath, / Shall be the worker of thy tragedy" (2. 1. 87, 91–93).

sword in the cellarage scene calls forth suggestions of Christian values and purposeful action based upon the ghost's revelations (for example, the hero's announcement of the antic disposition to be assumed)—in short, all the associations basic to that role of noble revenger in which many readers prefer to cast their favorite protagonist. But the near violence of act 1, scene 4, the presence of the ghost beneath the stage, and the general hellish-diabolic overtones (whether serious or antic) keep in front of us an alternative possibility—that the oaths and the sword may be associated with the black, destructive revenge envisaged by the orthodox, that the questionable ghost rather than Hamlet is truly in control of the situation. As with so many other moments in this play, the oaths and stage business of the cellarage scene suggest a dual potential in that sword to which our eyes are inevitably drawn. Is it to be a weapon that will set the time back in joint or one that will taint or poison its wielder? Is the antic mood of Hamlet's remarks an indication of his conscious control or of the ghost's effect upon him and his sword? No answers are provided here. Rather, the closing scenes of act 1 raise some challenging questions and in the process call attention to the sword as a meaningful, operative dramatic image. The groundwork has been laid for further development.

Hamlet's sword does not play a significant role in act 2 or the opening scenes of act 3. An attentive audience may catch various verbal references to weaponry; Fortinbras has promised no more "assay of arms" (2. 2. 71), while Rosencrantz reports that in the city "many wearing rapiers are afraid of goose-quills and dare scarce come thither" (343–44). But Hamlet's own weapon is not called to our attention, largely because the hero at this point is avoiding open combat, using indirections to conceal his new truths and find directions out. Rather, the dramatic image of the revenger's sword is developed through the appearance of the bloody Pyrrhus as described by Hamlet and the First Player at the end of act 2.

As pointed out in the previous chapter, Pyrrhus is described as a hellish revenger, covered with blood, roasted in wrath and fire, "o'er-sized with coagulate gore." Even "the whiff and wind of his fell sword" (473) are enough to overwhelm the old Priam whose "antique sword, / Rebellious to his arm, lies where it falls, / Repugnant to command" (469–71). This ornate description of revenge by the sword with its heavy emphasis upon blood forestalls any sympathy for the wielder of the weapon and prepares us for Hecuba's final vision of Pyrrhus making "malicious sport / In mincing with his sword her husband's limbs" (513–14). In this instance, revenge upon a king is bloody, brutal, malicious, and hellish.

As argued earlier, the verbal allusions to Pyrrhus's sword easily could be enhanced by stage business, for starting around line 477 ("for lo his sword . . . ") the First Player could not only declaim his lines but also mime the actions of Pyrrhus as he stands over Priam. The actor would only need a sword in his hand, a weapon that could be borrowed from Hamlet. Such staging would form an interesting link with the cellarage scene, for Pyrrhus's hellish use of his sword could reinforce one possible interpretation of the combination of Hamlet's sword, the oaths, and the ghost. To move further into the realm of conjecture, another player (with or without a crown) could mutely portray the kneeling Priam. Regardless, the behavior of the actor playing Pyrrhus is guided by the text, for, as noted in chapter 3, lines 477–82 demand that the revenger pause for more than ten lines with his sword poised in the air until the "now" of line 492 calls for its swift descent to mince Priam's limbs. Such staging would allow the viewer to hear *and* see Pyrrhus in action, first pausing over his aged and helpless victim and then following through in a manner that denies all sympathy to the act of revenge. As in the cellarage scene, the sword is associated with vengeance, with dire purpose, with killing a king, but the quasi-religious value suggested by the hilt-cross and the oaths has given way to the black purpose of the bloody, malicious, hellish Pyrrhus. This second appearance of the revenger's sword, therefore, should cause the audience to recall and reconsider that earlier dramatic moment when oaths sworn upon Hamlet's sword were urged on by "old mole" in the Hell beneath the stage. Hamlet's subsequent soliloquy is concerned with Hecuba, not Pyrrhus; obviously, he does not see himself or his sword in this particular "mirror up to nature." But the Player's speech can have a potent effect upon an audience that has noted in the Greek revenger a disastrous path that may be followed by a Danish son who feels compelled to kill a king with the sword of "a roused vengeance."

The first two scenes of act 3 contain scattered references to swords and weaponry. The "to be, or not to be" soliloquy includes not only the bare bodkin and the taking arms against a sea of troubles, but also, like the Player's speech, involves a significant "pause" that eventually gives way to talk of "action" (3. 1. 67, 87). Ophelia's description of the Hamlet she once knew cites "the courtier's, soldier's, scholar's, eye, tongue, sword" (151), while after the Mousetrap, Hamlet goes off to "speak daggers" to his mother "but use none" (3. 2. 396). But the next significant appearance of this dramatic image occurs at the pivotal point of the tragedy, the end of the prayer scene and the beginning of the closet scene, a critical moment that certainly qualifies as a watershed in Burke's terms.

To focus attention once again upon the revenger's sword, Shakespeare sets up the striking visual analogue noted in the previous chapter. During the Player's speech, Pyrrhus's sword "seem'd i' th' air to stick" but after that dramatic pause the "bleeding sword" fell on the helpless Priam. At the end of act 3, scene 3, Hamlet, not Pyrrhus, stands over Claudius, not Priam, but the visual analogy could be clear to the viewer. Hamlet, like Pyrrhus, starts off in the spirit of purposeful revenge (73–74) but then, again like Pyrrhus, pauses ("that would be scann'd").

After deciding that a better moment for revenge must be chosen, Hamlet puts up his sword (88), thereby apparently destroying the analogy or at least the equation of Hamlet with the bloody, hellish Pyrrhus. Yet Hamlet's desire for the damnation as well as the death of Claudius has seemed to some readers as black and hellish as Pyrrhus's motives, although the prince has paused and decided not to act when confronted with a kneeling, helpless antagonist apparently in a state of grace.

Hamlet's putting up of his sword after his pause in the prayer scene is but a prelude to the bloody use of that same weapon during the closet scene that follows, for here the prince not only drives his "words like daggers" into Gertrude's ears (3. 4. 95), but in a crucial action makes a pass through the arras that brings about the death of Polonius. Gertrude later describes the moment: "In his lawless fit, / Behind the arras hearing something stir, / Whips out his rapier, cries, 'A rat, a rat!' / And in this brainish apprehension kills / The unseen good old" (4. 1. 8–12). Just as Hamlet had failed to perceive the truth behind Claudius's façade of prayer, here he mistakes the reality behind the arras, crying out, "is it the King?" (26). As in the Player's speech, a thrust of the sword has killed an old man and tainted the swordsman.

Discovering his error, Hamlet provides a casual three-line epitaph for the "wretched, rash, intruding fool" and rushes headlong into a vehement attack upon his mother for her sexual sins. His obsessive diatribes that constitute the heart of the scene have fascinated Freudian critics and lay analysts, but little attention has been paid to visual effects and to the staging of these speeches. Any interpretation of the closet scene, however, is conditioned strongly by the decisions made about staging, particularly the positioning of Polonius's body and the disposition of Hamlet's sword. In most productions I have seen, Polonius's body is left behind the arras (so as not to distract the audience from the leading man's highly theatrical delivery of his emotion-packed speeches), while the sword is either left with the body or cast aside in the emotional confusion that follows. If the director does hide Polonius's body and shunt aside the bloody sword, he will enable the audience to retain their grasp upon the image of the noble Hamlet, the dedicated revenger, the dutiful son, the ponderer of the "to be, or not to be" soliloquy—the Hamlet who is not a Pyrrhus but rather the wielder of the quasi-religious sword suggested in act 1.

There is, however, an obvious and less pleasant alternative. What would be the effect upon an audience if the director left Polonius's body, covered with blood, in full view and left the sword, also bloodied, in the hero's hand throughout much if not all of the scene? An immediate result would be to force upon the viewer a series of ironic questions and juxtapositions. For example, Hamlet's announced purpose behind the speeches to his mother is the creation of "a glass / Where you may see the inmost part of you" (19–20), a mirror that will reflect her acts, her deeds, her crimes, the "rebellious hell" that "canst mutine in a matron's bones" (82–83). But how will an audience react to this account of Gertrude's crimes (largely against the memory of her first husband) if they are painfully aware of the body of Polonius, a bloody sword in the hero's hand, and a Pyrrhus-like stance on the part of the would-be revenger? As Eleanor Prosser frames the question, "Is it not terribly ironic that Hamlet, having himself just slain Polonius, should rage at the Queen for letting her blood master her judgment?"[16] Gertrude's original reaction to the murder ("O, what a rash and bloody deed is this!"—27) does not suggest an antiseptic presentation. If this emphasis upon blood and rashness is translated into appropriate stage business, what kind of evaluation of the hero is the audience forced into? Whose crimes at this point are more damaging, Gertrude's or Hamlet's? Without realizing it, Hamlet may be

16. *Hamlet and Revenge*, p. 194.

holding up a glass that shows the inmost part of himself, the "black and grained spots" upon *his* soul (89–91).

Once such ironic questions are raised for the audience, many of Hamlet's speeches take on added meaning. The emphatic presence of Polonius's body gives the hero's continual emphasis upon "such an act" and "such a deed" that "sweet religion makes / A rhapsody of words" (40–51) an unintended relevance to his own "rash and bloody deed." In the portrait speech, his repeated question "Have you eyes?" (65, 67), his attack upon his mother's "judgment" (70) and "quantity of choice" (75), and his assertion of her lack of "one true sense" (80) all can function as ironic comments upon his own blindness, lack of judgment, and rashness wherein "reason panders will" (88). Again, after the departure of the ghost Hamlet pleads:

> *Mother, for love of grace,*
> *Lay not that flattering unction to your soul,*
> *That not your trespass but my madness speaks;*
> *It will but skin and film the ulcerous place,*
> *Whiles rank corruption, mining all within,*
> *Infects unseen.*

$$[144–49]$$

Even though the audience, too, has heard and seen the ghost, Gertrude's diagnosis of madness in her son is supported by the presence of the body, the distracted use of the sword, and the casual disregard for the fate of the eavesdropper. Is Hamlet himself at this moment immune to his own strain of that "rank corruption" beneath the surface that "infects unseen" and destroys from within?

Such ironies, which may appear overly subtle to a reader, could be obvious to an audience visually aware of the body and the waving of a bloodied sword during the relevant speeches. As with the Player's speech, the effect easily could be attained and heightened by an actor and director conscious of the potential of this moment. Such a stage image is particularly meaningful when seen in its proper place as part of a larger pattern. Initially, the cellarage scene had suggested the dual potential inherent in the sword of revenge, but the first example of the revenger in action had been the hellish, totally unsympathetic Pyrrhus who first raised his sword, then paused, and finally followed through with the murder of an old man. Here in act 3 the central revenger of the play has raised his sword over Claudius, paused, put it aside, and a moment later made his pass through the arras to kill not the king but an old man not involved in the death of his father. In the closet scene, moreover, the sword of vengeance upon which oaths had been sworn appears again in the presence of the ghost. In act 1, scene 4, with the ghost on stage, that sword had been turned momentarily against two friends; in act 3, scene 4, the same weapon is stained with the blood of Polonius, perhaps a "wretched, rash, intruding fool" but scarcely deserving of this fate. In addition, the ghost's explanation that "this visitation / Is but to whet thy almost blunted purpose" (110–11) metaphorically defines Hamlet himself as a weapon that needs sharpening or redirection. Hamlet and his sword both have blunted their edge upon the wrong object.

The theatrical imagery occasioned by this suggested staging of the closet scene is of particular significance for the tragedy as a whole. In spite of Hamlet's many admirable qualities, his use of the revenger's sword (his first attempt at "action" after his "pause") has caused an unnecessary death that leaves blood on his hands, helps to drive Ophelia mad, and turns Laertes against him, thereby expediting both their deaths. Without realizing it, the tragic hero himself has been tainted with the disease and disorder of the world he has sought to cure, and the blood on his sword becomes an apt visual symbol for that stain or implication. For an audience sympathetic to the protagonist the striking analogy between the Player's speech and act 3, scenes 3–4, is particularly disturbing because the Wittenberg Hamlet of the famous soliloquy, the courtier described by Ophelia, the loving son and faithful friend, has unwittingly taken on many of the attributes of a Pyrrhus, a revenging son "roasted in wrath and fire" and "o'er-sized with coagulate gore." While Hamlet is setting up a glass for his mother in this pivotal scene, Shakespeare is establishing a larger mirror wherein the audience can view the inmost part of the distracted and now tainted hero. In several significant ways the sword's the thing by which the dramatist catches the conscience of the prince.

Significantly, there are no further references in the play to Hamlet's own sword, the weapon that killed Polonius. Before being brought to Claudius in act 4, scene 3, Hamlet is "guarded" outside (14), a term that would suggest his being weaponless. Later, Hamlet's letter to Claudius announces that "I am set naked on your kingdom" (4. 7. 43–44); "naked" has the potential meaning of "unarmed." The hero's one use of his weapon has stained the sword of act 1 with the blood of Polonius and thereby has symbolically eliminated that weapon as a potential tool for ordering the rotten world of Denmark. The next weapon we see in Hamlet's hands is a sword provided by his enemies, an integral part of the plot that will destroy him.

In contrast, Hamlet's two analogues who appear in act 4 are in obvious possession of their weapons. In act 4, scene 4, Fortinbras and his army, prepared for another "assay of arms," pass over the stage, acting out their readiness "to find quarrel in a straw / When honor's at the stake" (55–56). Then in act 4, scene 5, Laertes bursts into Claudius's presence waving his sword at the unarmed king. As Maurice Charney observes, "I don't see how this scene could be played without a sword or some other lethal weapon. There would be no terrors in a hand-to-hand wrestling match between Laertes and Claudius."[17] Again, the staging of this scene with its potential visual analogy to two earlier events is important. In his big speech Laertes cries out:

17. *"Hamlet* Without Words," *ELH* 32 (1965): 471.

"To hell, allegiance! vows, to the blackest devil! / Conscience and grace, to the profoundest pit! / I dare damnation" (132–34), clearly identifying himself with the Pyrrhus figure of act 2. But this determined revenger first is physically restrained by Gertrude (117, 123), then stunned by the appearance of the mad Ophelia, and finally manipulated by that same Claudius he had originally addressed as "vile king" (116). Once again a bloody, hellish, Pyrrhus-like revenger has raised his sword over an antagonist and then paused for a moment. Like both Pyrrhus and Hamlet, moreover, Laertes eventually acts after his pause, and that action taints both the revenge and the revenger.

The tool for the revenge so eagerly sought by this fiery youth is, not unexpectedly, the sword. In suggesting the fencing match, Claudius accurately predicts that Hamlet, who is "most generous, and free from all contriving, / Will not peruse the foils," thereby enabling Laertes "with ease, / Or with a little shuffling," to "choose / A sword unbated, and in a pass of practice / Requite him for your father" (4. 7. 134–39). Laertes, in addition, plans to touch his point or anoint his sword with an unction or contagion so that a slight gall will mean death to his opponent. Like the ghost in act 1, scene 5, Claudius here provides the facts about a father's murder to an injured son and urges revenge. But Laertes, unlike Hamlet, readily accepts the story told him by the wily king and never questions either the facts or the desirability of killing the supposed villain. In his quick acquiescence to the role of revenger thrust upon him by Claudius, Laertes has identified himself with and even helped to create the poisoned sword, a weapon with an obvious potential for corrupting both victim *and* wielder. This role of revenger-poisoner is just what Hamlet had sought to avoid (the ghost had enjoined him: "Taint not thy mind . . . "—1. 5. 85), but the rash and bloody murder of Polonius has already stained the sword of the cellarage scene. Significantly, the poisoned sword that will destroy Hamlet has been brought into being largely through the hero's misuse of his own weapon in the closet scene. The symbolic source of Laertes's poison is Polonius's blood.

The final and most telling appearance of this theatrical image is the poisoned sword of the fencing match, which serves as the climax to this tragedy. Shortly before that combat Hamlet describes the fate of Rosencrantz and Guildenstern and concludes: " 'Tis dangerous when the baser nature comes / Between the pass and fell incensed points / Of mighty opposites" (5. 2. 60–62). The two erstwhile friends are regarded as only minor casualties in a mighty duel between Hamlet and Claudius, a combat for the highest of stakes in which many bystanders are struck down. In retrospect, the duel metaphor aptly describes the battle of wits and stratagems waged since act 2. The plot of *Hamlet* is replete with feints, thrusts, parries, and counterattacks (for example, Claudius's use of Rosencrantz, Guildenstern, Ophelia, and Polonius; Hamlet's antic disposition and Mousetrap; the enforced trip to England; the secret death warrant and the changing of that commission), with various examples of "baser nature" being destroyed in the process (Polonius, Ophelia, Rosencrantz, Guildenstern, and eventually Laertes and Gertrude). Laertes represents Claudius's final weapon, while Hamlet's bated sword may serve as a comment upon his "almost blunted purpose." In a summary statement immediately preceding the fencing match that serves as dramatic climax, Shakespeare has given his audience a suggestive analogy between the duel and the central conflict of the tragedy.

In spite of its climactic position in this, the most widely discussed of all plays, the fencing match has received relatively little attention from scholars and critics.[18] Obviously, the duel was meant to be staged with much gusto both as an exhibition

18. A recent and notable exception is Nigel Alexander, *Poison, Play, and Duel: A Study in Hamlet* (Lincoln, Neb., 1971), especially pp. 173–74 and 194–95. For detailed discussions of the wager and the staging of the duel, see also Wilson, *What Happens in "Hamlet"*, pp. 276–90, and Harley Granville-Barker, *Prefaces to Shakespeare* (Princeton, 1946), 1:149–54.

of Burbage's swordsmanship and as a lively, theatrical climax to a long, weighty tragedy. Since the emphasis here is upon action rather than description or meditation, the dialogue lacks that imagistic fecundity that characterizes most of *Hamlet*; critics interested primarily in verbal or poetic effects have had little to say about this final scene, perhaps out of embarrassment at this nonintellectual ending to a highly contemplative play. But at this point in his career Shakespeare was at the height of his powers as a dramatist, and his creative imagination could encompass the full resources of the theater. After all the careful orchestration and development of sword imagery, an alert audience would certainly expect this final use of swords to be particularly meaningful and, in fact, to serve somehow as a key to the meaning of the tragedy. That audience would not be disappointed.

As in the cellarage or nunnery or closet scenes, the lack of stage directions or authentic stage traditions adds to the difficulties of interpretation, but still a definite series of events and actions can be set up from the text. When Osric brings forward the foils (259), Laertes looks for the unbated sword (264) while Hamlet, as Claudius predicted, is "free from all contriving" and does not examine closely the weapons offered him ("This likes me well. These foils have all a length?"—265). Laertes and Hamlet then play two bouts with Osric as judge, Hamlet winning both times (281, 286). After an inconclusive third bout (301), Laertes (whether in fair fight or through some treachery) wounds his opponent with the unbated, envenomed sword. Then, according to our one reliable stage direction from the Folio, "*in scuffling, they change rapiers.*" Because he has been wounded, Hamlet has realized that his opponent's weapon is unbated, and he has therefore forced an exchange of swords and inflicted a wound in return. Claudius's command ("Part them, they are incens'd") suggests a new mood not present in the earlier bouts, while Horatio points out that "they bleed on both sides." Dying from his own poison, Laertes announces: "Hamlet, thou art slain" and adds that "the treacherous instrument is in thy hand, / Un-bated and envenom'd. The foul practice / Hath turn'd itself on me"; he concludes: "The King, the King's to blame." Hamlet re-acts: "The point envenom'd too! / Then, venom, to thy work" as he stabs the king with the poisoned sword and a moment later forces the remainder of the potion upon his mighty opposite.

Although this tragic denouement has many significant fea-tures, perhaps the most important dramatic fact is easy to over-look, especially in reading rather than viewing this scene. For Hamlet is not only a victim of poison (as are his father, Gertrude, Laertes, and Claudius) but also a user of poison, a wielder of the poisoned sword. Just as the prince had fought back upon learn-ing of an earlier wound (the murder of his father), so here in his rage at an opponent's treachery he retaliates in kind and, already tainted with the contagion, himself becomes a poisoner.

Any reader sympathetic to Hamlet's dilemma immediately will raise several objections to this line of argument. The murder of Laertes is, of course, unintentional, for the hero does not know that the sword is envenomed until after the fatal blow; many readers see Hamlet's deliberate poisoning of the king as a decisive action at an opportune moment and therefore of credit to him. Nonetheless, Hamlet's unwitting *and* conscious wield-ing of the poisoned sword calls attention to a situation basic to his tragedy. Certainly an audience sides with the prince against Claudius and Laertes; Hamlet, we feel, should be the winner, should be able to cure the rottenness in Denmark, should be able to revenge his father. But throughout the play the world in which the hero must act is characterized by "seeming" surfaces, by baits of falsehood rather than carps of truth: Claudius's prayer is a sham; Polonius, not the king, is behind the arras; Laertes appears to be "a very noble youth" (5. 1. 224), not a poisoner. Hamlet then must carry out the ghost's injunction in a deceptive and poisoned world, a corrupted Denmark where "Offense's gilded hand may shove by justice" (3. 3. 58). To quote one of the most perceptive critics of the play:

The act required of [Hamlet], though retributive justice, is one that necessarily involves the doer in the general guilt. Not only because it involves a killing; but because to get at the world of seeming one sometimes has to use its weapons. He himself, before he finishes, has become a player, has put an antic disposition on, has killed a man—the wrong man—has helped drive Ophelia mad, and has sent two friends of his youth to death. . . . He had never meant to dirty himself with these things, but from the moment of the ghost's challenge to act, this dirtying was inevitable. It is the condition of living at all in such a world.[19]

The climactic expression of that "dirtying" is the poisoned sword, which is emphatically called to our attention by both Laertes ("the treacherous instrument is in thy hand") and Hamlet ("the point envenom'd too!"). As in the cellarage scene or the Player's speech or the prayer scene, all eyes for a moment are riveted upon that weapon; an actor need only pause and look searchingly at what he holds in his hand to heighten the effect. The fencing match therefore can serve as a symbolic summary of a major theme of this tragedy. Like Denmark as a whole, this supposedly friendly wager, this "playing" with swords, is not what it seems. Hamlet can win the first two bouts and draw the third; as he had told Horatio earlier ("I shall win at the odds"— 211–12), his skill as a swordsman is equal if not superior to that of Laertes. But because the fencing match, like the court, *is* corrupted or poisoned, Hamlet's individual prowess cannot produce the expected triumph. Rather, the final weapon in his hand provides a revealing comment upon his tragic error in the closet scene where a blind thrust through a seeming surface stained the revenger's sword with innocent blood. The foul practice has turned on Hamlet as well.

The poisoned sword, then, is a telling dramatic symbol for Hamlet's tragic involvement in a destructive and corrupting

19. Maynard Mack, "The World of *Hamlet*," *Yale Review* 41 (1952): 519. It is interesting how often critics speak metaphorically of the "weapons" Hamlet is forced to use without applying that metaphor to the duel that concludes the play.

world. The poison that has infected Denmark since King Hamlet's death has been purged, but not before the tragic hero himself has been affected by that contagion and has spread the final drops to the poisoners. At the climax of the play, the audience sees in Hamlet's hand not the ambiguous sword of the cellarage scene, not the bloodied sword of the closet scene, but rather "the treacherous instrument" created by the Pyrrhus-like son and the Machiavellian king. Hamlet does achieve his revenge and purge Denmark. But the instrument used in his final action is the poisoned sword of his enemies—a weapon forced upon him by necessity, which, though successful, symbolically expresses what the tragic hero has unwittingly (with Laertes) *and* knowingly (with Claudius) become—a poisoner. The Hamlet who is "most generous and free from all contriving" cannot achieve his ends in a corrupt world without himself partaking of that corruption. To set the time back in joint, a fatally infected Hamlet must be the final wielder of the poisoned sword.

Few readers will quarrel with my treatment of whisperers in *Woodstock* since the pattern uncovered only heightens the standard interpretation of the play. On the other hand, readers who reject the vision of Hamlet as tainted hero will be far less comfortable with my treatment of the poisoned sword. But my concern here is less with the interpretation than with the principles upon which it is based. Most important, *Hamlet* could be staged as suggested here with no omissions and no doctoring of Shakespeare's language or continuity. An actor about to create "his" Hamlet might prefer to see himself as the noble, philosophical Dane, but, without cutting or changing a line of the text, a director easily could make emphatic use of the sword imagery to present the less favorable view of the tragic hero. In fact, parts of the play often ignored by the critics (the fencing match) or omitted in performance (the Player's speech) are given added meaning through this approach. An uncut performance of *Hamlet* faithful to the text *could* realize the sword as a meaningful dramatic image for the viewer.

If the director or critic accepts my suggested staging, the presence of this image would be far more evident to an audience in the theater (then or now) than many of the iterative patterns established by more conventional criticism. In every act the revenger's sword makes a visually emphatic appearance: in the parapet and cellarage scenes of act 1; the Player's speech of act 2; the prayer and closet scenes of act 3; Laertes's arrival in act 4; and the fencing match of act 5. Certainly there is no shortage of verbal references to swords and weaponry. Without placing any severe demands upon the memory or attentiveness of the audience, this dramatic image can be operative and meaningful. To appreciate this image pattern, the viewer need only focus his attention upon the sword during the cellarage scene (where within a brief dramatic moment that weapon is central to the stage business and mentioned six times), recall that moment during the Player's speech (where the "lo" and "now" again draw all eyes to the sword), and then invoke that context in his evaluation of the prayer scene (where "up, sword" is another signal), the closet scene, and the fencing match. The sequence of the sword's appearances is one of the most compelling features of the pattern, for the accretion of meaning as the play develops is truly impressive, especially in the climax of the tragedy where the poisoned sword serves as a particularly revealing comment upon the dilemma of the tragic hero. Finally, in Burke's terms, there can be no question about the qualitative importance of an image emphatically set forth in the cellarage, closet, and duel scenes, moments that certainly correspond to his laying of the cornerstone, watershed, and valedictory.

My two examples of iterative theatrical patterns from *Woodstock* and *Hamlet* are obviously only a first step toward an authoritative treatment of Elizabethan dramatic imagery, just as my limited set of obvious symbolic actions can only suggest the potential in such moments. To explore or classify or even catalogue such imagistic or symbolic possibilities would take a sepa-

rate study. Rather, my goal has been to suggest the potential
rewards for the reader who can shed the spectacles of realism
and accept the importance of the viewer's eye, who can appreciate the richness of the poetry, yet look beyond the text to images
or actions that could be obvious and theatrically striking for an
audience. To do less is to rob Elizabethan drama and especially
the plays of Shakespeare of their third dimension—to encourage
a hostile ghost to come back from the grave to whet our almost
blunted purpose.

Chapter 5

The Obvious Fiction

In spite of the siren call of subtlety, my pursuit of the long-forsaken, much-maligned obvious in Elizabethan plays can be extended beyond imagery and symbolic action to the realm of dramatic irony. Certainly the critic, for whom "irony" and "ironic" are a way of life, need not be reminded of the value of literary juxtapositions and inversions. In the theater such effects are obvious when dramatist, director, and actors combine to play off what is said against what is seen. When Antony asks for reasons for the assassination of Caesar, Brutus's reply may seem relatively simple on the page ("Or else were this a savage spectacle"—3. 1. 223), but could have a far more complex effect to an audience looking at six or seven conspirators with bloody hands and bloody swords standing over a body bleeding from thirty-three wounds. Even simpler is the potential effect of Cassio's speech to Iago and the Cyprus gallants: "Gentlemen, let's look to our business. Do not think, gentlemen, I am drunk: this is my ancient, this is my right hand, and this is my left hand. I am not drunk now; I can stand well enough, and I speak well enough" (2. 3. 112–16). An added flavor would be provided if each reference to a motion or figure or condition is contradicted by Cassio's stage action; he could point to Montano rather than Iago, mix up his right and left hands, and end up stuttering and staggering. The total effect would be a simple yet forceful contrast between words and stage image.

By playing off a stage figure's limited or obtuse reaction

against an audience's visual experience, the dramatist can force his viewer to confront that figure's blind spots or follies, especially if the theatrical evidence (stage blood or obvious drunkenness) is emphatic. The consequent ironies are clear and unmistakable; no critical explanations are necessary. Since such a device can be a ready source of laughter, this technique is especially suited to comedy, as in the well-known scenes in *Much Ado About Nothing* where both Benedick and Beatrice are trapped into believing fictions evident to the audience. Perhaps the classic example is provided by Malvolio's entrance in act 3, scene 4, with his cross-garters, yellow stockings, simpering smile, and mistaken assumptions, all of which lead to the high comedy of cross-purposes when he quotes the letter and misinterprets Olivia's responses.

But such a technique can be used for more complex purposes, especially when the ironic interaction of words and stage image sets up issues or insights central to the play. Since his stage does not purport to present an illusion of reality, the Elizabethan dramatist can resort at times to an obvious fiction more elaborate than Cassio's speech, a fiction which may violate our modern notions of realism in order to establish some significant point. Such moments (the Dover Cliffs scene in *King Lear* is always the best example) often make the critic or director highly uncomfortable but nonetheless represent a striking and distinctively Elizabethan technique directed at the viewer's eye.

Consider as a point of departure act 4, scene 1, of *The Jew of Malta*,[1] especially the revealing interaction between the two visual symbols of Maltese Christianity, Friar Jacomo and Friar Barnadine. At the outset of the scene the two friars confront Barabas with his role in the deaths of Mathias and Lodowick. To sidestep such accusations, Barabas poses as a repentant Jew who has seen the error of his ways, asking: "Is't not too late

1. Text used is the RRD edition, ed. Richard W. Van Fossen (Lincoln, Neb., 1964).

now to turn Christian?'' (49); after tantalizing the friars with an elaborate catalogue of his wealth, Barabas concludes: "All this I'll give to some religious house, / So I may be baptiz'd and live therein" (74–75). In their intense competition for this apparent prize, the friars quickly forget the Jew's involvement in the deaths of two young men, thereby making a mockery of the vows of poverty supposedly basic to their profession. Ironically, the Christian ideal of giving up all worldly goods to a religious house in order to pursue one's salvation is placed in the mouth of a Machiavellian Jew who uses that profession to subvert the two obvious symbols of Christianity. Something is rotten in the state of Malta.

To underscore his point Marlowe now resorts to a visual analogue and an obvious fiction. With the departure of Friar Jacomo, Barabas and Ithamore have no difficulty strangling the sleeping Friar Barnadine (an action which may be a comment upon the sleeping if not defunct nature of Maltese Christianity). A moment later a second murderous attack is acted out, but this time the audience is offered the stage spectacle of a friar attacked not by the obvious infidels (Jew and Turk) but by a fellow Christian, Friar Jacomo. This dramatic duplication may seem unrealistic, given modern assumptions about dramatic economy and credibility. But in Marlowe's sardonic terms, Jacomo's violence acts out a second and more insidious threat—not from the grotesque outsiders but from forces within Malta, from the "Jewish" or "infidel" values shared by the Christians who duplicate the villainy of the Jew and the Turk.

To heighten the significance of this murderous duplication, Marlowe concludes the scene with an obvious fiction. Thus, after Friar Jacomo has been apprehended for his "crime," both Jew and Turk moralize about such evil deeds:

ITHAMORE: *Fie upon 'em! Master, will you turn Christian, when holy friars turn devils and murder one another?*

BARABAS: *No, for this example I'll remain a Jew.*
Heaven bless me! what, a friar a murderer?
When shall you see a Jew commit the like?
ITHAMORE: *Why, a Turk could ha' done no more.*

[4. 1. 189–94]

The viewer, unlike Jacomo, is aware of the truth behind the façade, having witnessed both murderous attacks, but the viewer
is also aware that the second friar *could* have been the culprit.
The fiction acted out by Barabas and Ithamore then has a curious
effect. Why should infidels "turn Christian" if the Christian
model held up for emulation is of such dubious value? What
fruits are to be found in Maltese faith, especially if holy friars
can turn devils? Jacomo's dilemma in no way exonerates Barabas
or makes the Jew's crimes palatable. But Marlowe *is* stressing
the essential similarity between the acknowledged Jew and the
supposed Christian who prides himself upon his superiority. As
Barabas puts it later in the play, "This is the life we Jews are us'd
to lead; / And reason, too, for Christians do the like" (5. 2.
115–16). To make his sardonic point, moreover, Marlowe has
resorted to an unrealistic yet theatrically potent combination of
visual analogue and elaborate irony, which produces a distinctive effect that is hard to classify.

Although subtler in tone and effect, Jonson uses the same
combination of visual analogue and elaborate fiction in act 4 of
The Alchemist. Earlier in the play Surly had pointed out that the
creator of the philosopher's stone "must be *homo frugi*, / A
pious, holy and religious man, / One free from mortal sin, a very
virgin" (2. 2. 97–99). Sir Epicure Mammon, however, assumes
that his "venture" can purchase the stone after such a saintly
figure "has worn his knees bare, and his slippers bald, / With
prayer and fasting for it" (101–4). For Mammon, the only problem is how to conceal his sensuality and obvious ineligibility for
the stone from the saintlike alchemist; thus he warns Surly:
"Here he comes, / Not a profane word afore him: 'tis poison"
(105–6).

But Doll's appearance in her mad fit at the outset of act 4, scene 5, is prima facie evidence of Mammon's sins to the supposed *homo frugi*. Upon his neatly timed entrance, Subtle comments upon Sir Epicure's "close deeds of darkness" (34), scoffs at his protestation that "there was no unchaste purpose" (37), and cites the inevitable results of such lustful action upon an alchemical process associated with purity and virtue (39–43). Mammon's patently false defense of his conduct ("our purposes were honest") is countered by the alchemist's rejoinder: "As they were, / So the reward will prove" (54–55). In his comic-satiric vein, Jonson has set up a test case whereby Sir Epicure's probity is to be judged or "proved" by his "reward," the outcome of the projection.

The results of this highly contrived test case follow quickly, for immediately after Subtle's line the audience is treated to *"a great crack and noise within,"* whereupon Face (as Lungs) rushes in to announce:

> O sir, we are defeated! All the works
> Are flown in fumo: every glass is burst.
> Furnace, and all rent down! As if a bolt
> Of thunder had been driven through the house.
> Retorts, receivers, pelicans, bolt-heads,
> All struck in shivers!
>
> [57–62]

At the news of such a heavenly thunderbolt, "Subtle *falls down as in a swoon*" (62 s.d.). When the alchemist *"seems come to himself"* (76 s.d.), he castigates "the curst fruits of vice, and lust!" and in his righteous indignation exclaims: "Hangs my roof / Over us still, and will not fall, O justice, / Upon us, for this wicked man!" (77–80). Mammon, who *has* been guilty of vice, lust, deeds of darkness, and a "voluptuous mind," is then "justly punish'd" (74), not only by Subtle's strictures but, far more painfully, by his enforced departure with no reward, no returns upon his investment, no fulfillment of his dreams of satisfaction and success. "Is no projection left?" he asks; "All flown, or stinks, sir" is the answer (89).

The audience, of course, is aware that Sir Epicure has lost only those visionary goals he had no chance of gaining in the first place (the philosopher's stone, Doll as a great lady); such visions of power and satisfaction have been encouraged by the "venture tripartite" only as long as they prove profitable (to them). But even though the explosion has accurately gauged Mammon's honesty, the audience also is aware that the figure of judgment (the supposed *homo frugi*) is as corrupt as his chastened victim. In a play replete with vice, stupidity, and crime, Jonson has provided this one example of the just retribution of the heavens upon man's deeds of darkness, but that retribution is obviously only another fraud perpetrated by the rogues to ensure their profit. That heavenly intervention repeatedly requested by Celia during the trial scenes of *Volpone* appears in *The Alchemist* but under dubious auspices; rather, here the viewer is forced to concede the spurious nature of that formulation, the transparency of the obvious fiction.

But Jonson does not stop here, for Surly's attempt to expose the rogues provides an alternative to Mammon's acceptance of the thunderbolt. When the gamester, still in his Don Diego costume, appears with Dame Pliant at the outset of act 4, scene 6, the audience is presented with the possibility that the conspiracy is about to be brought down by this shrewd, cynical figure, a human counterpart of the higher force that supposedly had destroyed the projection and Mammon's hopes. As in *The Jew of Malta*, moreover, a visual analogue helps to establish such a link. Thus, when Subtle attempts to pick the pockets of Don Diego, the alchemist instead is forced to "reel" (26) by an indignant (and well-informed) Surly. In contrast to the pretended swoon that had been used in the previous scene to gull Mammon, Subtle here, moments later, truly is struck down by an equally shrewd figure who has both learned the truth (elaborately catalogued in lines 35–54) and acted on the basis of that truth. Here, if anywhere, is the hope for that moral ordering so speciously applied to Sir Epicure, especially if the staging of Subtle's second fall to the stage floor recapitulates the first.

But the rogues, unlike the chastened Mammon, are unwilling to accept passively their just rewards. In the subsequent action, they successfully play upon the weaknesses of their victims (Kastril's desire to "give the lie," Drugger's dreams of winning Dame Pliant, Ananias's zeal) in order to create a comic uproar of fools and knaves that drowns out the unpleasant truth and drives it offstage. Surly's ejection is one of the most revealing moments in this play, especially insofar as it brings out the hollowness of the moral framework invoked against Sir Epicure. The gamester, who literally has brought the false alchemist to his knees, is the sole hope before Lovewit's return for any just retribution within the world of the play. Obviously, no thunderbolt carefully aimed from heaven is going to eliminate Subtle, Face, and Doll. Any such ordering must come from the responsible actions of individuals acting upon those principles so conveniently rejected in practice by the many figures Jonson has satirized. Both Jonson and Marlowe, each in his own distinctive way, have combined an obvious fiction with a linking analogue to indict the complacency of figures on stage and viewers in the audience.

Obviously, there are many different ways in which a dramatist can use his stage image to counterpoint or comment upon the words or assumptions of his dramatis personae. The test administered to Beatrice Joanna at the end of act 4, scene 2, of *The Changeling*[2] proves one thing to Alsemero (that his betrothed is "chaste as the breath of heaven"—149) but demonstrates something quite different to an audience that had observed Diaphanta also yawn, sneeze, and laugh in the previous scene. Alsemero's test becomes a comment not upon virginity but upon the deceptive power of surfaces; again, parallel staging

2. Text used is the Revels edition, ed. N. W. Bawcutt (London, 1958).

and an obvious pretense set up an extra dimension for the viewer. Or, to cite a well-known example, the glaring contrast between what the audience (and Ulysses and Thersites) sees in act 5, scene 2, of *Troilus and Cressida* and what Troilus is able to admit provides a major insight into the Trojan mind with its disdain for bounds and limits in its desire for the infinite.

The best examples of this technique are provided by two noteworthy scenes which are usually altered in modern productions to bring them in line with our realistic assumptions. First, consider act 4, scene 1, of *Othello*, which acts out the poisoned mind of the tragic protagonist. A few scenes earlier Othello had demanded "ocular proof" of Desdemona's infidelity, telling Iago: "Make me to see't" (3. 3. 360, 364). To accomplish this impossible task, Iago starts by pouring his pestilence into Othello's ear so that the evidence adduced will be distorted into the desired form (just as the evidence supplied by the letter causes Malvolio to twist Olivia's reactions in act 3, scene 4). Thus, Iago instructs the Moor:

> *Do but encave yourself,*
> *And mark the fleers, the gibes, and notable scorns*
> *That dwell in every region of his face,*
> *For I will make him tell the tale anew:*
> *Where, how, how oft, how long ago, and when*
> *He hath, and is again to cope your wife.*
> *I say, but mark his gesture.*

[4. 1. 81–87]

But when Othello withdraws to his vantage point, Iago tells the audience that he is going to question Cassio about Bianca, not Desdemona, a subject guaranteed to produce "excess of laughter." As Iago shrewdly observes, Cassio's smiles will drive Othello to madness because the Moor's "unbookish jealousy must conster / Poor Cassio's smiles, gestures, and light behaviors / Quite in the wrong" (101–3). In the moments that follow Othello observes the meeting between Cassio and Iago and the arrival of Bianca with the handkerchief, but since he does not hear what is said, he *can* construe the lieutenant's actions and gestures "quite in the wrong." The Moor's savage comments as he watches (for example, "O, I see that nose of yours, but not that dog I shall throw it to"—142–43) prepare us for his first response after Cassio exits ("How shall I murther him, Iago?"— 170). Thanks to the tempter's careful preconditioning, the tragic hero has received satisfying ocular proof.

Since this scene can be highly unpleasant for those who wish to retain their image of the noble Moor,[3] productions often omit the lines that reveal Othello's savage reaction to what he sees, while various devices are used to shift emphasis away from the eavesdropper. Like the Moor's brief appearance in act 5, scene 1, to cheer on a murder in the dark, this moment is not in keeping with the hero's self-image or with the stature attributed to him by some admirers. But that, of course, may be Shakespeare's point. The total effect of the scene, moreover, can be realized only if the audience is watching and listening to two actions on stage and is able to grasp the interplay between them. The true natures of Iago, Cassio, and Desdemona are clear to the viewer; during this scene, that viewer can hear the harmless remarks and understand the bawdy gestures that Cassio makes about Bianca. But Othello, on another part of the stage, cannot hear any such truth and, as a result, ends up distorting what he sees because of the poison Iago has poured in his ear; thus, Cassio's jokes and gestures can be translated into foul claims about Desdemona ("Do you triumph, Roman? do you triumph?"—118). Bianca's appearance is particularly signi-

3. For example, Harley Granville-Barker writes: "Othello is brought to the very depth of indignity. Collapsed at Iago's feet, there was still at least a touch of the tragic in him, much of the pitiful. But to recover from that only to turn eavesdropper, to be craning his neck, straining his ears, dodging his black face back and forth like a figure in a farce—was ever tragic hero treated thus?" After noting that most actors have avoided this scene, largely because it belittles the haughty and violent Othello, Granville-Barker adds: "The dodging in and out of hiding and the rest of the painfully grotesque pantomime is, of course, the most striking feature of the scene" (*Prefaces to Shakespeare*, 2:54).

ficant, not only because she brings in the handkerchief, but because Othello, in his tragic blindness, cannot distinguish between a real prostitute and Desdemona, whom he now sees in the same terms (an error that prepares us for act 4, scene 2, the so-called brothel scene).

Like Marlowe and Jonson, Shakespeare is taking great pains to set up an obvious fiction on stage, a fiction accepted by the deluded hero but evident to the audience. If the scene is played as written, the real subject or focus becomes not the degradation of the hero but rather the gap between what is truly happening and what Othello thinks is happening, the gap between what we see and hear and what the Moor sees and hears. Through this stage fiction, Othello can act out his poisoned mind, or, in other terms, the foul thoughts mentioned throughout the play are given dramatic flesh and blood. The fiction does not end in this scene, for in his famous "It is the cause" soliloquy of act 5, scene 2, the hero further develops this ironic double perspective on causes and evidence. But this telling moment displays to the audience the power of Othello's mind to transform virtue into pitch and to enmesh himself and those he loves in a net that will destroy them all. And the dramatist's tool for presenting this tragic delusion is the obvious fiction which deludes the observer on stage but has a far different effect upon the viewer.

The most complex example of the obvious fiction on stage is to be found in Gloucester's attempted suicide in *King Lear*, a scene that always has been a thorn in the side of critics and directors concerned with realism. Nineteenth-century productions spared their audiences any embarrassment at Shakespeare's naïveté by cutting much of the dialogue and by compressing the scene so that Gloucester could plunge forward (or be about to do so) only to be caught by Edgar, with Lear entering at that moment to interrupt their action.[4] Although modern critics and directors usually avoid such doctoring of the text, behind most essays or productions still lurks the assumption that a real fall or a symbolic representation of such a fall (if only from one raised step) is necessary to sustain the dramatic illusion and make sense of Gloucester's acceptance of Edgar's lesson.

But consider our only firm evidence, the dialogue that opens the scene:

GLOUCESTER: *When shall I come to th' top of that same hill?*
EDGAR: *You do climb up it now. Look how we labor.*
GLOUCESTER: *Methinks the ground is even.*
EDGAR: *Horrible steep.*
      Hark, do you hear the sea?
GLOUCESTER: *No, truly.*
EDGAR: *Why then your other senses grow imperfect*
      By your eyes' anguish.
GLOUCESTER: *So may it be indeed.*
      Methinks thy voice is alter'd, and thou speak'st
      In better phrase and matter than thou didst.
EDGAR: *Y'are much deceiv'd. In nothing am I chang'd*
      But in my garments.
GLOUCESTER: *Methinks y'are better spoken.*
$$[4.\ 6.\ 1\text{--}10]$$

Gloucester is being led to the place where he expects to renounce the world and shake his great affliction off by ending his life. His senses, which he no longer trusts, tell him that the ground is even, the sea is not nearby, and his companion is better spoken (an assertion repeated twice), but, as in act 2, scene 1, the old man is swayed by evidence or assurances provided by a son.

Many critics or directors choose to ignore or dismiss Gloucester's impressions. The blind old man can be led up an incline or across an upper level during this dialogue, with the emphasis placed upon Edgar's explanation that the "other senses grow imperfect" because of the "eyes' anguish." But Edgar here *is*

4. See Arthur Colby Sprague, *Shakespeare and the Actors* (Cambridge, 1944), p. 293.

better spoken than in act 3 or even in act 4, scene 1, where his speeches directed at his father (as opposed to those directed at the audience) retained the Poor Tom idiom (for example, 4. 1. 52, 54, 56–63). Given the accuracy of Gloucester's hearing in this instance, can we safely reject the old man's assertion that "the ground is even"? What would happen to this scene if we could rid ourselves of suppositions about heights and inclines and instead accept the data provided by the figure who is living this experience (as opposed to the assurances of the son who admittedly is trifling with his father's despair in order to cure it)? Since the Quarto stage directions tell us almost nothing (at line 34 "*He kneels*," at line 41 "*He falls*"), a nonrepresentational staging which provides no indication of height would be conservative, not radical; instead of adding to the text it would subtract insertions made by critics, editors, and directors uncomfortable with an apparent violation of dramatic credibility.

Granted such a simple staging, what would an audience in the theater actually see and hear? At the outset, Edgar in disguise would lead Gloucester across a flat stage while at the same time telling his father that he is being led up to a dizzying height described in a much-admired speech (11–24). The blind Gloucester questions the obvious contradiction of what his other senses tell him but passively accepts Edgar's statements. We would then see the old man detach himself from his guide ("Let go my hand"—27), give Edgar a purse, send him away, kneel, give what he thinks is his final speech, and finally fall forward, presumably to the death he welcomes. But if the director has not resorted to a raised level or an incline or even one symbolic step, Gloucester's fall would be from a kneeling position to the ground on a perfectly flat stage. At this point Edgar, using a different voice and accent, would step forward to announce that "thy life's a miracle" (55) and offer a description of the supposed fall. Regardless of any change in voice, the continuity of Edgar's role would be obvious to the audience as would the fictional nature of the plummet from the cliff.

What then is the effect of this suggested staging with no concessions to realism? The primary result is that the viewer is *forced* to confront the obvious fiction set up by Edgar and accepted by his father, a fiction clearly formulated in the moralization drawn from the "miracle" of Gloucester's survival. Thus, Edgar concludes:

> therefore, thou happy father,
> Think that the clearest gods, who make them honors
> Of men's impossibilities, have preserved thee.

[72–74]

To me, these lines are basic to any interpretation of the tragedy as a whole, with the phrase "think that . . . " of particular importance. In this tidy formulation, the blind old man is given an easy, satisfying, black-and-white opposition between the fiend who led him to the cliff (69–72) and the clearest gods who specialize in miracles that preserve mankind. Gloucester accepts this optimistic view, agreeing not to seek his death but to bear his afflictions (75–77). For the moment Edgar's device has worked; by deceiving his father in this way he has turned him from contemplation of suicide to "free and patient thoughts" (80).

But to stop with Gloucester's acceptance of the obvious fiction is to miss the full force of this moment. For the blind man's acquiescence to Edgar's miracle and to the role of the gods in that miracle is indicative of a significant strand of thought in this tragedy, a point of view best represented by Albany. Earlier, in his horror at the treatment given Lear, Albany had stated:

> If that the heavens do not their visible spirits
> Send quickly down to tame these vild offenses,
> It will come,
> Humanity must perforce prey on itself,
> Like monsters of the deep.

[4. 2. 46–50]

News of Cornwall's death resolves the question for Albany:

> This shows you are above,
> You justicers, that these our nether crimes
> So speedily can venge!
>
> [78–80]

Albany's conclusion ("This shows you are above . . .") is equivalent to the moral later accepted by Gloucester ("think that . . ."), but in both instances the audience is offered substantial evidence that such confidence in the positive intervention of the gods is misplaced. Even though the supposed speedy vengeance upon Cornwall is linked to the blinding of Gloucester, the others associated with that vicious action (Regan and Edmund) have so far suffered no setbacks and indeed are thriving. Albany, moreover, has just heard the messenger describe how not the heavens' "visible spirits" but rather "a servant that he bred, thrill'd with remorse, / Oppos'd against the act" had given Cornwall "that harmful stroke" (73–77). During the blinding, Gloucester had called out: "He that will think to live till he be old, / Give me some help! O cruel! O you gods!" (3. 7. 69–70) Neither this appeal for help nor the servant's intervention saved the old man's eyes, nor did the brutal action witnessed by the audience (including the killing of that servant) support Albany's conclusions about the justicers above. If anything, the servant's intervention is linked to Lear's exhortation based upon his experience in the storm:

> Take physic, pomp,
> Expose thyself to feel what wretches feel,
> That thou mayst shake the superflux to them,
> And show the heavens more just.
>
> [3. 4. 33–36]

In the highly suggestive final line, the king had implied that any justice from the heavens would be effected not through the obvious intervention of a divine thunderbolt but through the actions of men acting for the good of society (here "pomp," elsewhere the nameless servant, Edgar, Kent, Cordelia) who may somehow "show the heavens more just." The answer lies in human action, not in "a divine thrusting on" (1. 2. 126). Albany's confident formulation in act 4, scene 2, is thereby one of the many postulations about man and the gods tested and found wanting in this searching play.

The moral that Gloucester is persuaded to accept in act 4, scene 6, is then a restatement of the position consistently maintained by Albany. But, given a simple, nonrepresentational staging, the audience (unlike Gloucester) could not possibly accept Edgar's explanation of the miracle. Edgar (and Shakespeare) have placed the audience in a curious position. In questioning (or rejecting) the "miracle" and the moralization, the viewer is simultaneously questioning (or rejecting) Albany's confident assertions of act 4, scene 2, and the accompanying assumptions about heavenly intervention in man's affairs. The obvious fiction created by Edgar and accepted by Gloucester *prevents* the audience from sharing that comforting illusion. The bogus miracle then forces an attentive viewer to examine the mentality that can accept, even welcome, such an oversimplified explanation.

Edgar's presence at Dover Cliffs is more than mere coincidence; in spite of Gloucester's acceptance of an earlier fiction in act 1, scene 2, and act 2, scene 1, this son has chosen to follow and care for his father, here saving him from his own despair, later protecting him from Oswald. The true miracle is not Gloucester's survival from a nonexistent fall, but rather Edgar's meaningful assertion of the bond between child and father, a bond rejected by the blind parent but upheld by a loving son. At the outset of the play, Edmund had mocked his father's assumptions about the powers above ("an admirable evasion of whoremaster man, to lay his goatish disposition on the charge of a star!"—1. 2. 126–28). Here Edgar sustains that illusion in order to comfort his father, while he acts out for the audience a more realistic answer to man's dilemma based not upon the clearest gods or their visible spirits but upon human commitment.

Through this contrast between fiction and reality, Shakespeare has made it difficult if not impossible for a viewer to accept Albany's pat formulation or Gloucester's naïve faith in heavenly intervention. Meanwhile, Edgar's care for his father and his subsequent actions against Oswald and Edmund demonstrate that "to show the heavens more just" an individual must strive actively to right wrong, to act justly regardless of profit, to care for his fellow man, to create something out of nothing for the benefit of others. If the heavens are to play any role in man's affairs, that role somehow will be expressed through whatever force lies behind the bonds asserted by Edgar, Cordelia, and Kent, not through the type of miracle Gloucester has been persuaded to accept. Although "to think that the clearest gods" are striving actively for truth and justice in human affairs may be comforting, the reality is more complex and less convenient. Gloucester's blindness during this scene is again symbolic, not of his failure to understand his true son (as in acts 1 and 2) but of his inability to grasp the true role of the gods. That blindness, that acceptance of the obvious fiction, is certainly a comment upon Albany. Perhaps it is a comment upon us all.

Although my examples of obvious fictions do not form a neat pattern, each dramatist has presented some important point in theatrical italics by displaying a clear disparity between the credulity of a figure on stage and the awareness of the viewer. To note the presence of this device is not necessarily to argue for radically new interpretations of the individual plays, for the obvious ironies often clarify for an audience the same issues that the critics have already developed for the reader, whether the hypocrisy of the Maltese Christians or the twisted values of Face's London or the poisoned mind of Othello or the naïve faith of Gloucester. But given such striking moments for the viewer's eye, especially on the uncluttered, open stage, such interpretations can be realized for audiences not well-versed in scholarly literature or drama survey courses. Then or now, the obvious fiction can jar or move or enlighten the viewer.

Chapter 6

The Stage Psychomachia

My discussion of Elizabethan drama and the viewer's eye so far has skirted a major area of concern for the critic and the director —the presentation of "character." The director or theatergoer needs no reminder of the assets of theatrical presentation here. The dramatist in any period has advantages in displaying his characters that are not available to the novelist or poet, for the actor playing the role has recourse not only to words but also to gestures, tone of voice, facial expression, costume, and stage properties. Nonetheless, the Elizabethan dramatist could draw upon resources or conventions that easily can be missed by the critic or director coming to the plays with the assumptions of realism. Here is another area where the historian can provide contextual information not readily available to the modern reader.

"Psychology" or "character" in Elizabethan drama is a particularly thorny issue on which historian, critic, and director easily can come to blows. Even though studies of the four humours and melancholy are now out of fashion, scholars continue to expound upon such Elizabethan lore and then apply their findings to the drama in ways alien to modern expectations. For example, Madeleine Doran reminds us that, in the Renaissance, "critical theory taught that the persons of fiction and drama should be represented in their typical aspects" rather than as distinctive individuals. Although few historians would use such evidence to deny the individuality of a Hamlet or an

Othello, the theoretical statements of the age apparently pointed in a different direction.[1] Similarly, the modern reader can distinguish readily between psychology and moral philosophy as separate concerns, but such a distinction might have surprised many Elizabethans. Thus, James D. Redwine, Jr., argues that even if Jonson's humours theory "begins with psychology, it gets rather quickly into moral philosophy, where (one supposes) it was headed all the time." To Redwine, "the real subject of Jonson's theory of humours is neither psychology nor aesthetics, but moral goodness."[2]

Awareness of Elizabethan beliefs or assumptions need not prevent the critic or director from dealing in his own way with Hamlet's conflict. Shakespeare, it can be argued, was not constrained by the limited formulations of contemporary theorists, but was able to recognize and depict internal forces and psychological states in that piece of work, man, long before they had been categorized and codified. Yet the Elizabethans also may have developed their own distinctive methods for demonstrating character in action, methods which may elude the heirs of Ibsen. Thus, the analogue that links Hamlet to Pyrrhus does not resolve the various problems posed by his character but does place him in a continuum in which his actions could be more meaningful and understandable. Once again the historian is faced with limited external evidence and inadequate stage directions, but the wealth of information about at least one device—the stage psychomachia—suggests both widespread use and a lively potential for the viewer's eye.

1. See *Endeavors of Art*, p. 231, along with the entire chapter on "Character" (pp. 216–58). In a recent and very suggestive study, J. Leeds Barroll attempts with some success to wed the competing claims of historical scholarship and modern psychology; see his *Artificial Persons: The Formation of Character in the Tragedies of Shakespeare* (Columbia, S.C., 1974).
2. "Beyond Psychology: The Moral Basis of Jonson's Theory of Humour Characterization," *ELH* 28 (1961): 325, 330. For a discussion of the limitations of psychological analysis based upon humours (and also rhetorical archetypes), see Barroll, *Artificial Persons*, pp. 22–35.

Used in a dramatic context, the term "psychomachia" calls to mind the conflict found in the morality play in which a figure representing Mankind is torn between the blandishments of a Vice and the godly admonitions of a Virtue. Thus, in the most highly developed extant example (*The Castle of Perseverance*), "the subjective forces that in reality belong to man himself in the most personal sense were transformed by the poet into visible, external forces operating upon man as they obeyed, on the one hand, the call of God, or, on the other, the interests of the World and the Flesh." In this fashion, "the motives and impulses of man's own heart were taken from him, and, clothed in flesh and blood, given him again for companions."[3] Or, in A. C. Bradley's terms, the morality dramatists deployed their stage figures "to decompose human nature into its constituent factors."[4] By giving external stage life to man's internal forces, such a technique could use the special advantages of the theater to provide psychological insights and moral lessons; a verbal tirade against one or more vices clearly cannot match the theatrical vitality of a rambunctious Riot or a lascivious Lady Lechery.

In many fifteenth- and early sixteenth-century moralities, this psychomachia conflict served as the organizing principle which gave an entire play its distinctive shape. But by the 1560s and 1570s relatively few plays were built around a central figure like Mankind or Everyman. In his extensive treatment of the problem, Bernard Spivack argues that "the original metaphor" of the psychomachia had been disorganized in the late moralities so that "the personifications of vice and virtue" had been dispossessed "from their original function." For Spivack, the decline of the psychomachia is linked to the rise of the Vice, for "whereas the older moralities were about man, the later ones are about the Vice."[5]

3. E. N. S. Thompson, "The English Moral Plays," *Transactions of the Connecticut Academy of Arts and Sciences* 14 (1910): 315.
4. *Shakespearean Tragedy* (London, 1904), p. 264.
5. *Shakespeare and the Allegory of Evil* (New York, 1958), pp. 305–6.

Certainly, by the second half of the sixteenth century, the psychomachia no longer served as the dominant organizing principle for the morality play. But such an observation can obscure the other uses to which dramatists could put this technique—in particular, how within a given scene (rather than throughout an entire play) it could set forth a moral-psychological conflict in a meaningful and highly theatrical fashion. To appreciate the efficacy of this dramatic device, one must divorce it from the more general conception of "psychomachia" usually assumed. To do so here, I propose to narrow my focus and consider what I term the "stage psychomachia"—a dramatic moment in which a figure about to make a significant decision is on stage with two or more figures who in some way act out the alternatives involved in that decision. Through such a stage psychomachia, the terms of a major choice within the character's mind can be given dramatic flesh and blood.

An excellent early example can be found in *The Interlude of Youth*[6] (1520). In the first scene of this short play, Youth rejects Charity (who is dressed as a clergyman) and embraces (figuratively and probably literally) first Riot, then Pride, and finally Lady Lechery. As Youth, Riot, and Pride are about to depart for the tavern, Charity reenters and is both outnumbered and outfaced by the two vices. Youth has few lines in this scene (he is interested primarily in getting to the delights of the tavern and Lady Lechery); rather, the dramatic emphasis is upon the exhortations of Charity and the gibes of Riot and Pride; the climax is the placing of the virtue in the stocks. Left alone on stage, Charity can only lament the unstable, changeable nature of youth, pointing out "how vice is taken, and virtue set aside" and how man has used his God-given "wit and grace" only to choose such things "that his soul should spill" (p. 28). The stage image of virtue in the stocks, as T. W. Craik has pointed out, "is wholly symbolic of Charity's powerlessness in a mind where

6. Text used is Dodsley, 2:1–40.

Riot holds sway.'''[7] Before the eyes of the audience, the figure of virtue has been physically and verbally overpowered by his two opponents and then incarcerated, while the youthful protagonist has made his choice clear by exiting (probably arm in arm) with the two vices.

The conversion scene at the climax of the play provides an interesting contrast. Here Charity and Humility contest with Riot and Pride, a more equal match, and Youth at least listens to the virtues. Although the protagonist tells the vices that "I will be ruled by you two" (p. 31), the argument among the four allegorical figures is finally resolved in favor of the virtues, the clincher being Charity's account of how Christ sacrificed his blood to save Youth and all mankind. At this point, first Pride and then Riot exit, while Youth kneels, receives new array and devotional beads, and is promised an inheritance of bliss. Through dialogue, stage business, and visual imagery the dramatist is thereby giving external stage life to the forces within Youth's mind. The stocking of Charity and the exit with the vices act out the mind behind the protagonist's initial choice; in contrast, the exits of the vices singly, the domination of the stage by the virtues, and Youth's kneeling all display at length his final decision. Twice in this short play the dramatist uses the stage psychomachia to underscore his message and to extend theatrically the process of choice so that an audience can gain the fullest possible understanding.

Subsequent dramatists rarely make such extensive use of the stage psychomachia. Nonetheless, the technique was available in the early Elizabethan period for scenes involving important choices. Consider, for example, R. B.'s *Apius and Virginia*[8] (1564), a curious combination of tragedy and morality play. After Apius agrees to the Vice's plan (which will wrest Virginia from her family), the stage direction tells us: "*Here let him make*

7. *The Tudor Interlude* (Leicester, 1962), p. 94.
8. Text used is the MSR edition, ed. Ronald B. McKerrow and W. W. Greg (1911).

as though he went out and let Conscience *and* Justice *come out of him, and let* Conscience *hold in his hand a lamp burning and let* Justice *have a sword and hold it before* Apius' *breast"* (500). Although Conscience and Justice have no lines while Apius is on stage, the judge himself supplies their half of the argument:

> *But out I am wounded, how am I divided?*
> *Two states of my life, from me are now glided,*
> *For Conscience he pricketh me contemned,*
> *And Justice saith, judgment would have me condemned:*
> *Conscience saith cruelty sure will detest me:*
> *And Justice saith, death in the end will molest me,*
> *And both in one sudden me thinks they do cry,*
> *That fire eternal, my soul shall destroy.*
>
> [501–8]

Haphazard the Vice, however, mocks Conscience and Justice, arguing that "these are but thoughts" (510); he concludes: "Then care not for Conscience the worth of a fable, / Justice is no man, nor nought to do able" (521–22). Apius readily agrees to dismissal of his scruples ("let Conscience grope, and judgment crave, I will not shrink one whit / I will persever in my thought, I will deflower her youth"—525–26) and exits with the Vice. Alone on stage, Conscience and Justice then lament Apius's decision in psychological terms. Conscience complains: "I spotted am by willful will, / By lawless love and lust, / By dreadful danger of the life, / By faith that is unjust" (538–41), while Justice laments that "filthy lust" has "suppressed my virtues in one hour" (549–50).

R. B.'s choice of dramatic method to enact this major decision is suggestive and instructive. Somehow, at the moment when the judge is leaving the stage under the influence of the Vice and his own lust, Conscience and Justice are to "come out of" Apius, whether from behind his cloak or through some stage device (as in the genealogy of sin sequence in *All for Money*). The theatrically emphatic presence of these two figures (with their striking entrance, their emblems, and their gestures) is then linked verbally to Apius's own conscience and sense of justice. Although outnumbering the Vice, the two figures do not speak for themselves until after the protagonist's departure; in contrast to Haphazard's proximity, they could be physically distanced from Apius after their emergence or ignored. Apius's exit then can stress visually how he has abandoned his conscience and sense of justice in favor of his lust. Although to modern tastes this scene may not seem sufficiently "psychological," an early Elizabethan dramatist chose this method to dramatize the pivotal decision in his play. The curious stage direction which indicates that Conscience and Justice are to "come out of" Apius and the Vice's insistence that "these are but thoughts" provide interesting evidence of R. B.'s self-conscious use of the stage psychomachia to portray the inner workings of the mind of his protagonist.

Use of the stage psychomachia need not be limited to the fateful decision of a central figure like Apius. Thus, late in *The Tide Tarrieth No Man*, Wastefulness, one of a group of figures corrupted by the Vice, enters *"poorly"* (1660 s.d.) after squandering all his goods and treasure. Despairing, he tells us:

> *I know it is folly unto God to call:*
> *For God I know my petition will shun,*
> *And into perdition I am now like to fall.*
> *Despair, despair.*
> Despair enter in some ugly shape,
> and stand behind him.

[1678–81]

In the highly conventional dialogue that follows, Wastefulness cites the mercy mentioned in the Bible, but Despair argues that such pleas are all in vain and that the only rest is through suicide. Overwhelmed, the despairing figure announces that he will "seek some place where I may, / Finish my life with cord, or with knife" (1690–91). The stage direction tells the actor to *"feign a going out"* (1693), at which point Faithful Few, who has been a silent observer on stage, *"plucketh him again"* and offers the homiletic alternative—a critique of rashness, a reminder of God's mercy, and a call for faith and repentance (1694–99). The two figures then kneel (1700 s.d.), pray for mercy, and ask God to banish "that wicked monster of Despair," at which point *"Despair flieth, and they arise"* (1709 s.d.). Wastefulness now knows himself to be safe, for "Despair is now fled, I perfectly know, / And in God's mercy I firmly do trust" (1714–15).

This relatively brief moment from a play with many such episodes offers little that is doctrinally or psychologically new; treatments of Faith versus Despair are commonplace throughout the sixteenth century. But the staging of this traditional conflict here *is* interesting and suggestive. For example, Despair's ugliness, as specified in the stage direction, could have a distinctive effect upon the viewer; thus, when Wastefulness in his anguish calls out "Despair, despair," the entrance of such a loathsome figure could produce a striking effect in both theatrical and psychological terms, an equivalent to Conscience and Justice coming out of Apius at a critical moment. That Despair is to *"stand behind"* a figure who is denying the possibility of God's mercy and thinking of suicide stresses the internal dynamics of this psychological-spiritual force, while Wastefulness's decision to commit suicide "with cord, or with knife" could be heightened theatrically by having Despair (in conventional fashion) hand these two instruments to his victim. The attempted exit of the despairing figure (*"feign a going out"*), which leaves Despair dominating the stage, and the physical intervention of Faithful Few (who *"plucketh him again"*) display vividly the kind of stage contact that goes beyond mere allegorical description, while Despair's hasty departure after the kneeling in prayer acts out emphatically what has happened within the mind of the chooser (much like the exits of Riot and

Pride while Youth is kneeling in repentance). The simple yet forceful stage business (evident because of the unusually explicit stage directions) both heightens the psychological effects and acts out the interior state that can lead to despair and the Christian frame of mind that can counter it.

Such combinations of stage business and psychological allegory recur in early Elizabethan drama. Thus, in Lewis Wager's *The Life and Repentance of Mary Magdalene*[9] (1558) the key decision in the play (Mary's conversion) is handled in a similar way. On stage with the Vice (Infidelity), the heroine first is accosted by the Law of God (who carries tables of stone) and then by Knowledge of Sin, whom the Vice describes as "a pocky knave, and an ill favored; / The devil is not so evil favored, I think indeed, / Corrupt, rotten, stinking, and ill savored" (1112–14). Although Mary (encouraged by the Vice) at first resists her admonishers, she soon finds herself unable to pursue her life of pleasure because "this knowledge of sin is so in my sight" (1155). Perhaps pointing at the Vice, the Law exhorts her: "O sinner, from thy heart put that infidelity, / Which hath drowned thee already in the pit of hell" (1159–60). When Infidelity tries to discredit his opponents, Knowledge of Sin states:

> *Though I appear not to her carnal sight,*
> *Yet by the means that she knoweth the law,*
> *I shall trouble her always both day and night,*
> *And upon her conscience continually gnaw.*

[1219–22]

Eventually Christ forgives Mary's sins and drives out Infidelity and the seven devils that have possessed her. According to the stage direction, "Infidelity *runneth away*. Mary *falleth flat down*," while the devils cry "*without the door, and roar terribly*" (1302). The final lessons are provided by Faith and Repentance who

9. Ed. Frederic Ives Carpenter, the Decennial Publications of the University of Chicago, Second Series, vol. 1 (Chicago, 1904). I have modernized the spelling.

announce that "though in person we shall no more appear, / Yet invisibly in your heart we will remain" (1447–48). Like R. B. or Wapull, Wager has used groupings, exits and entrances, and stage imagery to develop his moral-psychological progression. The ugliness of Knowledge of Sin (like that of Wapull's Despair), the growing number of figures who confront Infidelity, and the physical expulsion of the Vice and the seven devils all combine good theater with psychological development.

Such moments are to be found in almost every late morality that deals with moral choice and moral error. For example, in *The Trial of Treasure* the dramatist provides consecutive scenes in which the Vice Inclination first controls the vicious Lust but in turn is controlled by the virtuous Just. In the latter scene, Just listens to the counsel of Sapience and bridles Inclination. The moral-psychological lesson is never in doubt ("thus should every man, that will be called Just, / Bridle and subdue his beastly inclination"—p. 279), while the staging and groupings reaffirm the alternatives facing Lust and Just. Similarly, the corruption of Worldly Man in *Enough is as Good as a Feast* follows the standard pattern. The protagonist, in simple array, enters with Enough but is quickly accosted by the Vice Covetous (dressed in considerable finery) and Precipitation. At first Worldly Man stands "*afar off*" (627 s.d.) with Enough, but gradually the Vice moves in and separates him from his original companion. When Worldly Man makes an attempt to rejoin Enough, the stage direction instructs Covetous to "*pluck him back*" (741 s.d.). After a verbal confrontation between the virtue and the vices has explored the different senses of "enough," the exit of Enough (866 s.d.) provides a visual key to the descent of Worldly Man who now can describe his former mentor as "a beggarly knave" (870); the final stage direction in the scene has the remaining three figures depart "*all three together*" (line 948), perhaps arm in arm. The psychological process displayed here is later summarized: "The unquiet mind of the covetous doth grutch and swell, / And to

live with Enough he doth abhor and detest. / The greedy grasp-
ing of Covetous doth him so molest . . . " (1502–4). Again,
entrances, exits, blocking, physical contact, and costumes are
used to make explicit the internal dynamics of a worldly choice.

Given the limited number of extant plays, five examples of
the stage psychomachia in the early Elizabethan period represent a substantial body of evidence. Clearly, the dramatists of
the 1560s and 1570s found this combination of stage effects and
psychological allegory useful for displaying internal conflicts.
But many changes took place in English drama over the next
two decades, so equivalent examples are harder to find in the
extant plays from the 1580s and 1590s. The stage psychomachia,
however, does persist. Thus, near the end of Lodge and Greene's
A Looking Glass for London and England[10] (1590) the usurer enters
"*solus, with a halter in one hand, a dagger in the other*" (2041–42).
After some twenty despairing lines, the stage direction tells us:
"*The evil angel tempteth him, offering the knife and rope*" (2064–65).
Unfortunately, the text provides no indication of how or when
this evil angel appears on stage nor is there any firm evidence
for the presence of a good angel. Yet the usurer, after listening to
the voice of despair, states: "What second charge is this? /
Methinks I hear a voice amidst mine ears, / That bids me stay:
and tells me that the Lord / Is merciful to those that do repent"
(2068–71). After hearing this second voice (and somehow rejecting the halter and the dagger), the usurer "*sits him down in sack-
clothes, his hands and eyes reared to heaven*" (2078–79). Although
brief and underdeveloped, this scene does show the survival of
the dramatic convention, particularly if two angels and appropriate stage business are invoked.

Another example is provided by *A Warning for Fair Women*
(1599) where a pivotal event, the seduction of Mistress Sanders,

10. Text used is the MSR edition, ed. W. W. Greg (Oxford, 1932).

is presented not by a realistic temptation sequence but by an allegorical dumb show.

next comes Lust *before* Brown, *leading* Mistress Sanders *covered with a black veil:* Chastity *all in white, pulling her back softly by the arm: then* Drewry, *thrusting away* Chastity, Roger *following: they march about, and then sit to the table: the* Furies *fill wine,* Lust *drinks to* Brown, *he to* Mistress Sanders, *she pledgeth him:* Lust *embraceth her, she thrusteth* Chastity *from her,* Chastity *wrings her hands, and departs:* Drury *and* Roger *embrace one another: the* Furies *leap and embrace one another.*

[D1 recto]

Acting as presenter, Tragedy explicates this dumb show for the audience, placing particular emphasis upon the conflict within Ann Sanders between Lust and Chastity:

> *Thus sin prevails, she drinks that poisoned draught,*
> *With which base thoughts henceforth infects her soul,*
> *And wins her free consent to this foul deed.*
> *Now blood and Lust, doth conquer and subdue,*
> *And Chastity is quite abandoned:*
> *Here enters Murder into all their hearts,*
> *And doth possess them with the hellish thirst*
> *Of guiltless blood:*

Here again, as in the morality plays, significant stage business (for example, the thrusting away of Chastity, the embracing of Lust) can serve as a dramatic shorthand to make explicit for the viewer the psychological forces at work.

The best-known survival of the stage psychomachia is, of course, to be found in *Doctor Faustus*. Marlowe's use of the good and evil angels has provoked a great deal of reaction, much of it unfavorable, but as Wilbur Sanders has pointed out, "Far from being clumsily primitive, this is an immensely dramatic procedure. The first effect of the interruption is to arrest all action on the stage, and to focus attention on the protagonist, suspended in the act of choice. Not until he speaks do we know to which voice he has been attending. It is the act of choice in slow motion, a dramatisation of his strained attention to the faint voices of unconscious judgment."[11] Although Sanders is discussing only one scene, his observation applies equally well to other parts of this tragedy and, indeed, to other Elizabethan plays, early and late. A technique directed at the viewer may seem primitive to the reader until it is realized on the stage. Thus, to the critic nurtured on Henry James, the stage psychomachia may seem a blemish in an otherwise complex tragedy, but in the theater such a suspension or slowing down of the process of choice may be a worthy equivalent to the novelist's presentation of interior states of consciousness.

Although the surviving stage directions offer little help, there are many ways to enhance Marlowe's stage psychomachia. Upon his first appearance, the good angel exhorts Faustus to "lay that damned book aside" and instead "read, read the scriptures" (scene 1, lines 69, 72); here the heavenly figure could offer a Bible to a Faustus immersed in his book of necromancy ("How am I glutted with conceit of this!"—77), perhaps Jerome's Bible rejected earlier, while the spirit or evil angel (perhaps deformed in appearance like Despair or Knowledge of Sin) either offers his own book or urges Faustus on in his reading. During their second appearance, one angel calls upon Faustus to "think of heaven and heavenly things," the other to "think of honour and of wealth" (scene 5, lines 21–22); again, a Bible could be played off against gold or jewels. During the third such scene, Faustus momentarily thinks about repentance (scene 6, lines 10–11), hears the two angels ("God will pity thee. . . . God cannot pity thee"), and comments: "Who buzzeth in mine ears I am a spirit?" (12–14). The reference to buzzing or muttering suggests an intimate physical relationship between the protagonist and the two embodiments of his inner conflict (reminiscent of Despair standing behind his victim). Near the end of the tragedy the two angels enter *"at several doors"* (scene 19, line 98 s.d.), a puzzling stage direction which could indicate either a

11. *The Dramatist and the Received Idea* (Cambridge, 1968), p. 217.

new method of entry or one followed throughout the play. Moments later the evil angel probably would exit through the trap or hellmouth, to be followed at the end of the scene by Faustus himself who has made his choice and must follow that course. In contrast, the good angel, who is associated with the heavenly throne and with forces above, probably would exit in some appropriate fashion. Such exits and entrances, as in the morality plays, could heighten Marlowe's distinctions or alternatives in moral-psychological terms.

Admittedly, discussion of the stage psychomachia cannot resolve the many problems posed by Marlowe's tragedy. The modern reader cannot even ascertain whether Faustus actually hears the speeches of the two angels (for example, turning his head to attend to the different voices) or whether his attention is focused upon his books or his infernal pact (a staging that would stress the internal nature of the voices). Regardless of the choice made by critic or director (I prefer the latter), Faustus's moments of decision, as Sanders points out, have been slowed down in a theatrically effective manner that heightens the internal conflict. Both tension and clarity are well served by such a device, which could have a potent effect upon an audience not far removed from the plays of R. B., Wapull, and Wager. If the two angels do act out their appeals in elaborate, physical terms, a viewer could gain a far greater appreciation of the moral geography of Faustus's mind.

At least one other play provides suggestive evidence about the survival of the stage psychomachia in the 1590s. Thus, Launcelot Gobbo in *The Merchant of Venice* has a speech of some thirty lines clearly based upon the psychomachia model. In his comic debate with himself over whether or not to run away from Shylock, Launcelot sets up two opposing forces, Conscience and the Devil, and then summarizes their arguments. Each voice has its own lines and perhaps its own gestures, for in high comic fashion the clown plays both parts (and, of course, himself in the middle). Much of the fun undoubtedly arose from Launce-lot's (or Will Kempe's) varying postures and inflections as he acted out the strictures of Conscience or the insinuations of the Devil, perhaps to the point of leaping back and forth when he reached "Bouge" versus "Bouge not." At the end, the clown is back in the middle, pointing to both sides:

"Conscience," say I, "you counsel well." "Fiend," say I, "you counsel well." To be rul'd by my conscience, I should stay with the Jew my master . . . and to run away from the Jew, I should be rul'd by the fiend. . . . my conscience is but a kind of hard conscience, to offer to counsel me to stay with the Jew. The fiend gives the more friendly counsel: I will run, fiend; my heels are at your commandment, I will run.

[2. 2. 19–32]

No one can be certain how this scene was staged in the 1590s, but surely much of the comic effect depended upon the parody of a well-known stage convention, which would be far more effective if based upon recognizable stage business (such as opposing stances, contrasting postures, even contrasting voices), not just a general model.

Doctor Faustus is the only major play of the 1590s to present psychomachia conflicts in which psychological forces are neatly labeled by means of angels or allegorical personae. What then are we to conclude about the staging of internal conflicts in primarily literal drama? Are the techniques found in the morali-ties or in *Doctor Faustus* no longer workable or fashionable for later dramatists and audiences? Or do similar techniques persist but in a manner following the prevailing dramatic winds? By 1600, has the psychomachia on stage suffered an eclipse or undergone a metamorphosis?

Years of conditioning to realism would cause most modern readers to accept the former possibility. *Doctor Faustus*, then, constitutes a memorable backward look at an older, outdated technique. But the obvious popularity of Marlowe's play, as evidenced by its lively stage history (at least into the 1620s) and the succession of editions (including the significant 1616 B text), should forestall such an easy dismissal. Moreover, two curious passages from Jonson's later plays also challenge our automatic assumptions about realism. Thus, in the opening scene of *The Devil is an Ass* Satan gives Pug, the inept devil, a scornful lecture about the difference between old-style devils and vices (of 1560) and those of today (1616). Nowadays, "they have their Vices, there, most like to Virtues; / You cannot know 'hem, apart, by any difference" (1. 1. 121–22); the Vice of the morality play, according to Satan, would be helpless against the up-to-date techniques of Meercraft and his cohorts. The distinction between 1560 and 1616 is not in kind (vices or Vices are still relevant) but in subtlety or fashion. Similarly, in *The Staple of News* (1626) Tattle associates the Vice with his traditional attributes (a wooden dagger, a devil to carry him off), but Mirth contrasts "the old way" to the current fashion in which such figures "are attir'd like men and women o' the time."[12] Again, according to Jonson's spokesman, the Vice has not disappeared; rather, changes in dramatic taste and technique have caused him to shed his allegorical identity in favor of a role more suitable to the contemporary stage and society.

Both passages from Jonson suggest that the predominantly literal or realistic surface of seventeenth-century drama need not totally rule out techniques or effects originally associated with "the old way" that *did* use allegorical virtues and vices. To what extent do such possibilities apply to the stage psychomachia? To see the problems in answering such a question, consider Posthumus's crucial decision in act 2, scene 4, of *Cymbeline*. On one side stands Jachimo who offers convincing evidence of Imogen's infidelity, which appeals to the hero's baser nature; but also on stage is Philario, the voice of reasoned caution, a figure not in any of the numerous sources and analogues, whose presence makes

12. C. H. Herford and Percy and Evelyn Simpson, *Ben Jonson* (Oxford, 1925–52), 6:168, 323.

the chooser appear far less blameless. Although literal stage personae, both Jachimo and Philario *could* correspond to forces within Posthumus at this moment, an effect that *could* be heightened through staging and theatrical give and take. As usual, we can only guess at how the scene would have been staged. Jachimo and Philario could be physically involved with Posthumus (literally pulling him in opposite directions) or they could be positioned on opposite sides of the stage to draw attention to sharply divided alternatives. Jachimo's displaying of the bracelet and Posthumus's subsequent handing over of the ring suggest some physical contact, while Philario either could interfere ("take your ring again, 'tis not yet won"—114) or be progressively distanced from the figure who is succumbing to his tempter. For an early seventeenth-century audience not far removed from the obvious stage psychomachia, Posthumus's choice of Jachimo/slander over Philario/reason *could* have larger psychological resonance, especially if the literal staging follows theatrical patterns associated with the allegorical staging of the previous generation.

Obviously, the historian or critic must tread carefully here. Even if a potential exists for such a stage psychomachia, there need not be a larger psychological meaning in every scene in Elizabethan drama (and there are many) in which a figure making a decision stands between other figures who offer alternatives. Faced with such scenes, the reader must carefully weigh the evidence and the potential effect. For a negative example, we can turn to *The Shoemaker's Holiday* when Rafe, Hodge, and the shoemakers interrupt the marriage of Jane and Hammon. When Hammon asks if Jane will leave him, Hodge plays stage manager, telling Rafe: "set the wench in the midst, and let her choose her man, and let her be his woman" (5. 2. 49–52). Although a suspenseful pause could follow, there is no real conflict or slowing down of a mental process, for Jane makes her choice within three lines. Moments later, after Hammon has offered twenty pounds in gold for Jane, Rafe too makes his choice with dispatch. In both instances, the alternatives are clear: for Jane, wealth/position versus husband/love/duty; for Rafe, gold versus Jane. But Dekker's oppositions are thematic, not psychological. Unlike the earlier stage psychomachias involving Apius or Wastefulness or Faustus, there is little sense here of the theatrical and psychological give and take that can act out a mind at work.[13]

Outright examples of the literal stage psychomachia, however, remain elusive. Consider Kastril's dilemma in *The Alchemist* when Face and Dame Pliant are offering competing versions of the truth about Surly and the alchemical operation. Kastril and Face enter together, the latter feeding the angry boy a quickly concocted story about Surly's villainy (4. 7. 1–3, 8–11, 16–22). To defend himself against Kastril's insults and threats, Surly appeals to Dame Pliant ("Lady, do you inform your brother"— 15), but the angry boy accepts Face's version, thrusts away his sister ("Away, you talk like a foolish mauther"—23), and helps to drive Surly and the truth off the stage. Before or during the moment of decision, would Face and Dame Pliant be buzzing in Kastril's ear in a manner reminiscent of the angels with Doctor Faustus (who had just been mentioned—4. 6. 46) or would they be pulling the youth in different directions or perhaps fighting over his sword with Face urging him to draw it, Dame Pliant trying to restrain him? Although not a fully developed character like Faustus or Posthumus, Kastril *is* acting out the mentality that makes possible the success of Face and Subtle (for example, the choice of wish-fulfillment fantasies over a less-pleasing re-

13. Similarly, in act 1, scene 2, of John Ford's *Perkin Warbeck*, Lady Katherine is asked to choose between duty to her father, the Earl of Huntley, and affection for Lord Daliell. Huntley instructs Daliell: "Keep you on that hand of her, I on this," adding: "Thou stand'st between a father and a suitor, / Both striving for an interest in thy heart. / He courts thee for affection, I for duty" (94–97). But there is no real conflict here, for Katherine, pleading inexperience with the world, shows no true desire for her suitor but emerges as a model of duty (like Dekker's Jane). See the RRD edition, ed. Donald K. Anderson, Jr. (Lincoln, Neb., 1965), p. 18.

ality). Through the stage psychomachia (even in abbreviated form) Jonson could be displaying to his audience the mental processes of many of the gulls in this comedy. But such an effect would work only if backed up by groupings and stage business that recalled the traditional effect, and Jonson did not bequeath us any such stage directions.

Another problematic example is provided in *Arden of Faversham*[14] after Arden and Franklin have driven off Moseby, Will, and Shakebag. With Franklin at his side, Arden has defeated his enemies and recognized Alice as an "injurious strumpet" and Moseby as a "ribald knave" (scene 13, line 78). But when Alice reenters, Arden is unable to resist her explanation—that the apparently loving relationship between her and Moseby had been only sport, a merry jest to test Arden's patience. Franklin's objective appraisal ("Marry, God defend me from such a jest"—98) is ignored; rather Arden is totally deceived, even to the point of asking his wife for forgiveness and promising her that she will have her will "whate'er it be" (130–31). Franklin's final objection ("Why, Master Arden, know you what you do?"—135) is dismissed by the husband who states: "I pray thee, gentle Franklin, hold thy peace; / I know my wife counsels me for the best" (148–49). Alone on stage, Franklin observes that "he whom the devil drives must go perforce"; since Arden is bewitched by his own wife, "his friends must not be lavish in their speech" (152–55). Like Posthumus, Arden has rejected the voice of reason in favor of some baser appeal. Again, Arden's relationship to the two speakers easily could recall or build upon the stage psychomachia, especially if the staging of the scene shows Alice's sensual appeal having an obvious effect upon her husband while he is progressively distanced from his rational friend.

Other scenes with similar possibilities can be cited. During acts 2 and 3 of Shakespeare's *King John*, King Philip is forced to make key decisions while various figures around him (King

14. Text used is the Revels edition, ed. M. L. Wine (London, 1973).

John, Lewis, Pandulph, Constance, Elinor) argue for expediency or for right. In act 2, scene 1, of *The Revenger's Tragedy*, Gratiana faces the blandishments of Vindice/Piato on one side and the virtuous arguments of Castiza on the other. In act 3, scene 3, of *A King and No King*, Arbaces, in love with his sister Panthea, hears both the high-minded arguments of Mardonius and the debased insinuations of Bessus. In all three scenes, important choices are made between well-defined alternatives. Adept use of blocking, exits, and properties could enable such scenes to depict the forces at work within the chooser.

Perhaps the best example is to be found in act 3, scene 7, of *Antony and Cleopatra*. At the outset, Cleopatra and Enobarbus, the Egyptian queen and the Roman soldier, discuss her presence at Actium and its potential effect upon Antony. According to Enobarbus, "Your presence needs must puzzle Antony, / Take from his heart, take from his brain, from's time, / What should not then be spar'd" (10–12). Cleopatra, however, announces her determination as head of her kingdom to "appear there for a man." "Speak not against it," she tells the Roman, "I will not stay behind" (17–19). Thus, at the beginning of this crucial scene the Roman and Egyptian attitudes are associated with specific figures on stage and are developed at least partly in psychological terms (such as puzzle, heart, brain).

At this point Antony enters, talking with Canidius about military matters, dressed for battle, and undoubtedly *looking* like a Roman hero. But within a few lines Antony is arguing against his Roman compatriots and is allied with Cleopatra—a new grouping that surely would be reflected by the staging; thus, Cleopatra (like Alice Arden) probably would attach herself to Antony so that the two of them would face the Roman soldiers together. For much of the remainder of the scene Antony's decision to fight at sea is pitted against the rational, strategic arguments of Canidius, Enobarbus, and the soldier, all of whom act out the Roman point of view. But such arguments are countered by Antony's will ("By sea, by sea"; "I'll fight at sea"), by his response to Caesar's dare, and by Cleopatra's assertion that "I have sixty sails, Caesar none better" (40, 48, 29, 49).

Given the importance for the tragedy of this decision to fight at sea, this scene often appears underdeveloped to the reader. But in the theater, the total stage picture could be more potent than the dialogue, especially if Cleopatra is hanging upon Antony, visually puzzling him by her presence, clearly affecting his Roman manhood by taking from his heart, brain, and time what should not be spared. In Canidius's terms, "our leader's led, / And we are women's men" (69–70). Through the staging, Cleopatra's influence over Antony (as displayed in intimate physical terms) should be played off against his separation from the Romans who represent qualities or values demonstrably present in the hero but temporarily muted or overruled. Antony's exit arm in arm with Cleopatra, leaving behind three Roman soldiers, acts out symbolically and psychologically the choice he has made and bears out Enobarbus's later analysis that Antony made his will the lord of his reason and let the itch of affection nick his captainship (3. 13. 3–8). Here is a prime example of how the stage psychomachia can be used to explore in theatrical terms the mind of a tragic hero and to display the internal conflicts that set much of the play in motion.

Vestiges of the stage psychomachia can be found in the 1590s and even after 1600. Certainly, the historian can point to scenes in which a figure on stage must choose between other figures who represent moral or psychological alternatives. But my constant use of "may," "could," "perhaps," and "if" demonstrates how the shortage of evidence, especially the lack of adequate stage directions, makes firm conclusions impossible. The modern reader, therefore, is left with a difficult and perhaps unanswerable question: to what extent would an Elizabethan audience watching a chooser faced with two literal figures who act out alternatives have equated those figures with the internal forces behind the choice? Such a theatrical means for presenting and slowing down the workings of the mind was prevalent in the 1560s and 1570s and was workable (if a bit old-fashioned) as late as the 1590s. *If*, then, the stage psychomachia was linked firmly to specific staging practices (exits and entrances, group-ings, physical contact) and *if* those practices were carried over into the literal scenes of choice, the later scenes *may* have gained added resonance by drawing upon audience awareness of the earlier, more obvious allegorical technique. Ironically, the critic or director who finds such psychological meanings in *Cymbeline* or *Antony and Cleopatra* is not discovering something new but rather is resuscitating "the old way" (in Jonson's terms) of dealing with internal conflict on stage.

My discussion of the stage psychomachia so far has been limited to scenes in which an individual like Apius or Faustus or Antony acts out his choice between alternatives. There are, how-ever, other possibilities. Thus, a dramatist, using an equivalent technique, could set up a stage conflict so that the mind exhibited is not identified with one protagonist but rather with a larger group or entity. To the modern reader, such a technique may appear overly subtle, but the historian can point to early plays such as *Albion Knight* (1537) and *Respublica* (1553) that did use a larger entity—England—as a protagonist. Ironically, introduc-tion of a stage psychomachia into a later play to analyze a society would be not an innovation but an updating of an older technique.

Consider first act 4, scene 8, of 2 *Henry VI* in which the mob enters following their leader, Jack Cade, who has led them to victory after victory. But Cade is faced with a different kind of opposition when Buckingham and Old Clifford arrive with a pardon from the king for those rebels who will forsake their present leader and go home in peace. Clifford's first speech calls upon those who love the king to throw up their caps "and say,

'God save his Majesty!' " (15). The crowd complies. Cade answers with an impassioned speech that recounts all he has done for his followers. The mob responds: "We'll follow Cade, we'll follow Cade!" (33). But Clifford counters with the benefits offered by the king and then draws an elaborate picture of what the French will do to a divided England ("I see them lording it in London streets"—45). The crowd responds: "A Clifford! a Clifford! we'll follow the King and Clifford" (53–54).

A disgusted Cade sums up the political lesson provided by these responses: "Was ever feather so lightly blown to and fro as this multitude? The name of Henry the Fifth hales them to an hundred mischiefs, and makes them leave me desolate" (55–58). But the total theatrical effect easily could approximate the stage psychomachia. Thus, by placing Cade and Clifford at opposite ends of the stage with the mob in the middle, the subsequent movement back and forth and the responses to the alternating appeals could correspond to a protagonist's conflict between virtue and vice. This effect, moreover, would have ominous implications for the play as a whole and for the first tetralogy because the stage picture of a populace with such divided loyalties over an obvious fraud like Cade is an ominous prelude for the forthcoming threat of Richard of York whose abilities and claim to the throne are far more formidable. The specious arguments used here to sway the rebels and to thwart Cade will not apply to York in act 5, so the wavering mob on stage in act 4, scene 8, can display in theatrical terms the divided mind behind the civil wars to come. The stage psychomachia thereby has been adapted to a larger, yet still recognizable, purpose.

An even subtler adaptation of the stage psychomachia can be found in Malvolio's incarceration during act 4, scene 2, of *Twelfth Night*. Although the intended staging is unclear, the stage direction that Malvolio be *"within"* (20) suggests that the supposed madman is either offstage (with a stage door representing his prison) or within some discovery space at the rear of the stage or within some temporary boxlike structure carried on stage or thrust up through a trap door. Somehow, the hapless steward is imprisoned before our eyes and subjected to the elaborate trick played by his enemies. Thus, at the outset, Maria supplies Feste with a clerical gown and false beard which are donned quickly (Sir Toby's entrance line is "Jove bless thee, Master Parson"—11). For Malvolio's benefit, Feste changes his voice (Sir Toby tells us that "the knave counterfeits well"—19) and passes himself off as Sir Topas the curate. Thinking that he has found an ally, Malvolio complains that "they have laid me here in hideous darkness" (29–30), an assertion that should correspond to the visual evidence presented to the viewer, who should hear but not see the steward. In the exchange that follows (33–47), however, Malvolio's claims (for example, "I say this house is as dark as ignorance") are challenged by Feste/Sir Topas who instead posits the existence of clerestories and "bay windows transparent as barricadoes," concluding that "there is no darkness but ignorance, in which thou art more puzzled than the Egyptians in their fog." Malvolio is correct (he *is* in darkness, he is *not* truly mad), but nonetheless there is an ironic force in Feste's comments about the darkness of ignorance.

Malvolio's statement to the supposed curate that "I am no more mad than you are" (47–48) is soon followed by a similar pronouncement ("I am as well in my wits, fool, as thou art"—88) to a Feste who has now reverted to his own voice. The clown's rejoinder is typical of his *tu quoque* technique ("But as well! Then you are mad indeed, if you be no better in your wits than a fool" —89–90), wherein he serves as a touchstone to heighten the unacknowledged folly of others. But Malvolio's iterated claims about his sanity keep calling our attention to his mental processes; particularly striking is his final and most sweeping assertion that "I am as well in my wits as any man in Illyria" 106–7). Given the witless, obsessive behavior apparent throughout this comedy (summed up in the previous scene by Sebastian's confused question: "Are all the people mad?"—4. 1. 27), Malvolio's claims here can be highly suggestive. Through such statements the steward *thinks* he is establishing his own sanity by equating the state of his wits with the general norm in Illyria. Yet for an audience alert to such possibilities, he is actually doing just the opposite—stressing his own comic madness and calling attention to how he is acting out in extreme form a malady that has reached epidemic proportions in the world of the play. Throughout *Twelfth Night* such comic madness or bedevilment has been associated with the failure to distinguish between similar objects (Viola and Sebastian, Olivia's and Maria's handwriting) or with the willingness to allow appetites or self-indulgence to distort reality (Orsino's "love" for Olivia, Malvolio's wrenching of the letter, Olivia's statement to Cesario that "I would you were as I would have you be"). In his real and symbolic darkness-madness here in act 4, scene 2, Malvolio can serve as a dramatic emblem for the Illyrian state of mind.

In one of the funniest moments in the play, Shakespeare then provides a striking display of this state of mind through a device related to the stage psychomachia:

CLOWN: *Advise you what you say; the minister is here.—*
Malvolio, Malvolio, thy wits the heavens restore! En-
deavor thyself to sleep, and leave thy vain bibble babble.
MALVOLIO: *Sir Topas!*
CLOWN: *Maintain no words with him, good fellow. —Who, I,*
sir? Not I, sir. God buy you, good Sir Topas. —
Marry, amen.—I will, sir, I will.
MALVOLIO: *Fool, fool, fool, I say!*
CLOWN: *Alas, sir, be patient. What say you, sir? I am shent for*
speaking to you.

[94–104]

For a few lines Feste thus plays both himself and "Sir Topas" in rapid succession. Undoubtedly he adjusts his voice to confuse

Malvolio; perhaps he takes off his beard and gown as he switches roles, or perhaps he moves from one place on stage to another for each set of lines. The quick change or quick movement (or both) needed for the "Marry, amen" and the "I will, sir, I will" could be extremely funny, especially if the final switch to the curate's costume has the beard awry or the gown on backward or if Feste does not quite have time to complete the change.

But to note only the comic business is to miss the larger effect, an effect related to both the stage psychomachia and the obvious fiction. Earlier in the scene, after Feste first had impersonated Sir Topas, Maria had remarked that "thou mightst have done this without thy beard and gown, he sees thee not" (64–65). If Malvolio is in darkness and cannot see, there is no realistic need for this disguise. But the larger effect of the scene is based not so much upon the trick itself as upon the disparity between the reality accepted by Malvolio and the truth recognized by the audience. What the viewer *sees* is some form of cell from which emanates a voice that complains of darkness and equates its level of sanity with all of Illyria. At a climactic point the viewer *sees* that the figure (or mind) behind this voice cannot distinguish between a fool (who in costume and behavior represents a constant for the audience) and a fool disguised as a curate (a potential figure of virtue and order, especially for a Puritanical steward). The disembodied voice (divorced from the physical presence of the actor) and the verbal emphasis upon wits and madness heighten the psychological dimension of the scene; meanwhile, the theatrical presence of the cell (regardless of which staging is used) provides a convenient emblem for the mental bondage to illusion and self-love that is being acted out. In short, Feste's Sir Topas disguise is for our benefit, not Malvolio's. The high comic presentation of the two voices and the two roles sets up for us the terms of the steward's malady—a darkness of ignorance that can confuse religion and folly so that the higher self is imprisoned. This cell, moreover, is a potential trap awaiting many other figures in the comedy who in their own distinctive ways cannot distinguish between sheer folly and some supposedly loftier pursuit; in particular, the spurious Sir Topas could provide an interesting equivalent to the idolatrous religion of love practiced by Orsino and Olivia and parodied by Sir Andrew. Granted, there is no obvious stage psychomachia here wherein Malvolio stands between two figures who represent opposing forces in an inner conflict, but in a related fashion Shakespeare is providing a remarkable display of the state of the steward's mind, which in turn epitomizes the distinctively Illyrian brand of self-deception and comic madness.

An equally interesting variation on the stage psychomachia is to be found in act 2, scene 2, of *Troilus and Cressida*, the much-discussed Trojan council scene. Careful readers already have shown how this scene orchestrates the Trojan values that eventually lead to the deterioration and ultimate demise of an entire society (as symbolized in act 5 by the death of Hector and the disillusionment of Troilus). Relatively little attention, however, has been paid to the staging of this scene. As a point of departure, consider the stage picture presented to the viewer. Priam, who introduces the topic for discussion (1–7), is certainly on his throne—an old, revered king who should be the symbol of order and control. But with the exception of a brief comment to Paris later in the scene (142–45), Priam says nothing, leaving the fate of Helen and Troy in the hands of his sons. He could be listening intently, following the alternating speakers with his head; he could be frozen in place; he could even be napping. Regardless, as king-order-reason figure he remains on stage (as does Helenus the priest) not as an active force but as a representation of qualities or faculties that are ineffectual.

In contrast to Priam's passivity, the audience sees, on one side, two young men, Troilus and Paris, who argue vigorously in terms of will, appetite, and honor and, on the other side, Hector, who for much of the scene speaks out for reason and moderation. The arguments back and forth would be particularly effective if the factions were on opposite ends of the stage with Priam in the middle as a subdued order figure; a viewer thereby could be seeing as well as hearing a display of the Trojan mind at work throughout the play, a mind that constantly reaches out for the infinite and boundless and disdains the confines of reason or limit. Cassandra's brief but startling appearance midway through the scene, with her prophetic vision of the disaster to come, calls our attention to what is at stake ("Troy burns, or else let Helen go"—112). But the obvious pivotal moment comes at the end of Hector's long speech on the "moral laws of nature and of nations" (184–85) when he announces:

> Hector's opinion
> Is this in way of truth; yet ne'er the less,
> My spritely brethren, I propend to you
> In resolution to keep Helen still,
> For 'tis a cause that hath no mean dependence
> Upon our joint and several dignities.

[188–93]

Here and in his speech that ends the scene (206–13) Hector's values cannot be distinguished from those of his "spritely brethren," regardless of what has gone before. The effect indeed would be puzzling if the subject of the scene were Hector's train of thought, for Shakespeare provides no evidence for the switch from the way of truth to the way of honor. But the focus here is upon the mind of Troy, not the mind of Hector; like Priam's passivity, the hero's about-face is not primarily an end in itself, a display of "character," but rather a means to a larger end—a demonstration of the vulnerability of reason and truth to the siren call of honor in the Trojan mind. Clearly, during either of his final speeches, Hector would cross the stage to join Troilus and Paris, thereby breaking the visual image of reason standing off will and appetite (with Paris a particularly good embodiment of the latter). The simplicity of the *"Exeunt"* which denotes the end of the scene cloaks many possible striking effects. For example, Troilus, Paris, and Hector could stride offstage, arm in arm, while an aged, decrepit Priam is slowly helped off by an ashen-faced, tight-lipped Helenus. Or all five figures could depart together in some way that would undercut the stature and dignity of Helenus and particularly of Priam. The protagonist here has been no one character but Troy itself. For more than two hundred lines the most fateful decision in the play has been slowed down and physically acted out so that a viewer can fully grasp the larger mind behind it. As with the incarceration of Malvolio, Shakespeare again has used a variant of the stage psychomachia to give theatrical flesh and blood to a state of mind basic to his play.

There are, of course, other ways to present on stage the mind or general attitude of an entire society. The use of choric figures is common in classical drama; the moralities provide figures like Common's Cry and Common's Complaint (*Cambises*) or Vulgus (*Patient and Meek Grissill*) or People (*Respublica*); one thinks of the king's molehill speeches in *3 Henry VI* or the Chorus in *Henry V*. But the presentation of the mob's reaction to the speakers in *2 Henry VI* takes a significant step beyond such choric summaries by using the resources of the theater to enact a conflict and its resolution. Or, to cite another example, the shifting of seats by the senators in act 5 of Jonson's *Sejanus* sums up visually both the switch in allegiance away from Sejanus and the heliotropic values of Tiberius's Rome. The particular advantage of the stage psychomachia as adapted in *Twelfth Night* and *Troilus and Cressida* is that the specific ingredients of the larger mind at work can be displayed to the viewer in the theater. Particularly in *Troilus and Cressida* (as in *Doctor Faustus* or *Antony and Cleopatra*), the viewer attuned to such possibilities could come away with a far better understanding of the mind behind a key decision than would the reader limited to the printed page.

In a suggestive passage, Bernard Beckerman has used the series of Shakespearean scenes involving eavesdropping or concealed observation to characterize dramatic conventions. Once we recognize this device as a convention, we become conscious of how the dramatists could "select dramatic activity from artistic tradition, thereby gaining readily accepted dramatic tools." Such a convention builds upon "theatrical practice not life activity," for "the observation scene is an artificial formulation, obeying its own rules, following its own forms, and judged according to its own context."[15]

My purpose in this chapter has been to document another Elizabethan dramatic convention, one far less noticeable to the modern reader than is the observation scene. To borrow Beckerman's terms, I have been concerned with a dramatic tool drawn from the sixteenth-century theatrical tradition, which undoubtedly was known and appreciated in the age of Shakespeare but may be obscured today. To see the potential in this tool, the critic or director first must recognize it as a convention and then grasp its distinctive rules and forms, thereby weighing dramatic practice over life activity. To achieve this end, my discussion has wound its way through materials of limited interest to the critic and director, but such byways often can lead to greater understanding of major works of art, especially for the reader relatively unfamiliar with the Elizabethan terrain. The critic may disagree with my treatment of Malvolio or the Trojan mind, but my argument at least should establish that such effects were within the range of mature Elizabethan drama, a historical point of some importance. My concern is with what Elizabethan dramatists were doing and what they *could* do.

In plays ranging from *The Interlude of Youth* to *Antony and Cleopatra*, the sixteenth- and early seventeenth-century English dramatists could draw upon a common fund of material in their native tradition to present states of mind or moral conflicts in a

15. *Dynamics of Drama* (New York, 1970), p. 26.

nonrealistic, nonrepresentational manner that had its own psychological complexity, its own theatrical vitality. Although modern assumptions about realism and psychology may prevent our full appreciation of such a technique, still the potential *was* there, especially for a dramatist of Shakespeare's caliber able to use his theatrical legacy effectively and imaginatively. Only when we take into account this significant part of the Elizabethan dramatic heritage can we fully account for the psychological dimension of the plays in the age of Shakespeare. To do less is to stage our own psychomachia—to have Everyreader exit arm in arm with Oversimplification while Reason and Truth are left behind.

Chapter 7

Conclusion:

The Viewer's Eye
and the Spectacles of Realism

By this point, the reader may have had enough of my obvious fictions and theatrical decisions. My cast of critic, director, and historian, moreover, may be ready for a Pirandello-like rebellion against the script I have chosen. Clearly, the distinctions among such personae cannot be pursued too far. The critic is often a director in the theater of his mind wherein he can generate ideas and possibilities that can be translated to the stage; while any successful production is essentially an essay in criticism, with the director's interpretation realized through actors, action, and dramatic time rather than through ink and paper or the lecture platform. Regardless of my distinctions and regardless of any running quarrels, critic and director share many common goals and interests.

But the historian's potential contribution is less obvious (and perhaps less welcome). Let us recall Bernard Beckerman's observation that "each time a reader takes up a copy of a play, he also puts on a pair of spectacles" with lenses "compacted of preconceptions about what constitutes drama and how it produces its effects." Because such spectacles are unseen and unacknowledged, their power to distort can be especially strong; thus, the modern reader, not recognizing his preconceptions, can blithely assume that there is but one way to read a play, one way to look at drama. But if we heed the historian, we can recognize that there are differences, both obvious and subtle, between our conception of drama and that implicit in Elizabethan plays. Once conscious of our spectacles, we can take a fresh look at the original "language" built into these plays. Although the reader may not wax enthusiastic over all the techniques or examples cited in this study, there *was* a potential in the age of Shakespeare for linking analogues or theatrical imagery or symbolic actions or obvious fictions or stage psychomachias, devices that can yield an extra dimension to our appreciation of both major and minor plays. More examples and devices are undoubtedly there to be rediscovered once the modern reader sheds his unhistorical spectacles.

At least one major component of these misleading spectacles should be singled out, for every good story needs a villain. If our hero is Everyreader searching for Truth, the major villain is Realism, that complex of expectations and assumptions about character, plot, and overall logic brought to Elizabethan drama by the modern reader nurtured by the novel and the mainstream of drama since Ibsen. As I have argued again and again, many of my examples draw their force from violations of realism: the horseboy in *Edward II*; Heywood's supernumerary Maid; the puppetlike behavior of Francis the drawer; Falstaff or Barabas or Altofront rising from the dead; Gloucester's "fall" at Dover Cliffs; Feste's unnecessary disguise; Hector's about-face in the council scene. Expectations about realistic action and behavior can inhibit our understanding of many, even most, Elizabethan plays.

Although the reader may be weary of this argument, I would like to cite one last example. The 1974 summer season of the Oregon Shakespearean Festival included a highly successful rendition of *Titus Andronicus* directed with imagination and precision by Laird Williamson. The acting was strong; the staging often was stunning; the violence was stylized and very effective.

Only two scenes in this problematic play continually evoked unwelcome responses (usually embarrassed laughter) from the audience: the "fly" scene (3. 2.) and the scene in which Quintus and Martius are trapped in the bloody pit. The "fly" scene may pose insuperable difficulties, for here the gap between Elizabethan and modern tastes may be too great to bridge, but the "pit" scene, in my opinion, *could* work on the modern stage although not in realistic terms.

Here are the lines leading up to the central action (these lines were pared down somewhat in the Ashland production):

MARTIUS: *O brother, help me with thy fainting hand—*
If fear hath made thee faint, as me it hath—
Out of this fell devouring receptacle,
As hateful as Cocytus' misty mouth.

QUINTUS: *Reach me thy hand, that I may help thee out,*
Or wanting strength to do thee so much good,
I may be pluck'd into the swallowing womb
Of this deep pit, poor Bassianus' grave.
I have no strength to pluck thee to the brink.

MARTIUS: *Nor I no strength to climb without thy help.*

QUINTUS: *Thy hand once more; I will not loose again,*
Till thou are here aloft or I below.
Thou canst not come to me—I come to thee.
Falls in.

[2. 3. 233–45]

Consider first the logic of realism. The director reasons that this moment is meant to demonstrate the failure of one brother (Quintus) to pull another (Martius) out of a hole in the ground. Therefore, if the audience is to believe in the attempt and the failure, they must have a sense of the depth of the pit and the difficulty of the task. The director thereby placed Martius out of sight beneath the stage (with the result that his lines were muffled) and had Quintus on his knees reaching down into the trap (with the result that some of his lines and most of the action were lost to the viewer). Such a staging satisfies the logic of realism. But the scene fails. The audience sees only the ignominious, unintentionally funny fall of the second brother with no apparent point at stake. The viewer is left shaking his head in wonder at Shakespeare's lapses early in his career.

But if we could shed the spectacles of realism, what alternatives could we see here? Obviously, the moment acts out a failure to save a fallen figure, which climaxes with a second fall into the same trap; the emphasis in the dialogue (and implicitly in the stage business) is upon hands ("help me with thy fainting hand"; "reach me thy hand"; "thy hand once more"). To resuscitate this scene, the director must have the hands not only visible but central to the action. Consequently, Martius, the brother in the pit, *must* be visible, perhaps even from the waist up, regardless of any realistic logic to the contrary. Quintus then could be standing, not kneeling (again regardless of realism), so that the viewer's eye would be trained upon the linked hands

Tamora pleading to Titus Andronicus for the life of her son. This drawing in a manuscript usually attributed to Henry Peacham (author of The Compleat Gentleman) *may reflect a performance in 1594 or 1595. The manuscript is in the library of the Marquess of Bath at Longleat; it is published with permission of Lord Bath.*

(as with God and Adam in the Sistine Chapel), a bond between brothers that fails and brings down the would-be rescuer.

To appreciate fully the failure of this bond, the reader must be conscious of the patterned presentation of hands, limbs, and bonds throughout the tragedy, ranging from the lopped limbs of Alarbus (1. 1. 97, 143) to the broken limbs of Rome that eventually must be knit together again (5. 3. 72). Particularly important is our view of the maimed Lavinia, who enters in her mutilated state soon after this moment at the pit, and the self-maimed Titus, who sacrifices his own hand to no avail in act 3, scene 1. Although hands are not mentioned specifically, much of the force behind these moments is initiated by Tamora's plea for the life of Alarbus:

> *Stay, Roman brethren! Gracious conqueror,*
> *Victorious Titus, rue the tears I shed,*
> *A mother's tears in passion for her son;*
> *And if thy sons were ever dear to thee,*
> *O, think my son to be as dear to me! . . .*
> *But must my sons be slaughtered in the streets*
> *For valiant doings in their country's cause?*
> *O, if to fight for king and commonweal*
> *Were piety in thine, it is in these. . . .*
> *Thrice-noble Titus, spare my first-born son!*
>
> $\left[\text{1. 1. 104–20}\right]$

Throughout this study, I have lamented the lack of external evidence, especially detailed accounts of specific performances, but for this moment the historian can provide an illustration from the 1590s, the so-called "Peacham drawing."[1] According to

---

1. See the accompanying illustration. For an excellent reproduction of the drawing and text along with valuable commentary see S. Schoenbaum, *William Shakespeare: A Documentary Life* (New York and Oxford, 1975), pp. 122–23. Another bit of suggestive external evidence is provided by a Frenchman, Jacques Petit, who saw a private production of *Titus Andronicus* during the 1590s and commented that the show was of more value than the subject (*la monstre a plus valeu q le suiect*). See Gustav Ungerer, "An Unrecorded Elizabethan Performance of *Titus Andronicus*," *Shakespeare Survey* 14 (1961): 102–9.

this illustration, the focus for this pivotal scene is the figure of Tamora, kneeling in supplication, her hands together to accent her plea for her son's life. This stage image of a kneeling, pleading figure could be repeated several times in the long opening scene as various characters present their pleas before first Titus and then Saturninus. But Tamora's plea (and her hands) fail, and that failure is associated with the family ties denied by Titus in favor of the "Roman rites" (143) cited by Lucius and encouraged by his father. In symbolic terms, then, the failure of hands and of family ties acted out by Quintus and Martius or by Titus himself in act 3, scene 1 (when he offers his hand to save the lives of these same two sons) does have a dramatic logic, even a compelling dramatic logic, because Titus and his sons are suffering in terms linked to their earlier barbaric treatment of Tamora and her son. If Martius in act 2, scene 3, is in full view, so that the emphasis for the viewer is upon hands and not solely upon the fall, the larger effect could be striking, obvious, and highly meaningful, an integral part of the original language of the play that has been obscured by modern spectacles. The search for realism here leads only to embarrassment, but the resurrection of the original logic could give back to this moment its force and meaning.

For the modern reader, *Titus Andronicus* may seem a poor example with which to conclude. The problems posed here for the director or critic (in this moment or the arrow-shooting scene or Tamora's masquerade as Revenge) are not to be found in *Hamlet* or *King Lear* or *Othello* where our sense of credibility or character apparently suffers no such setbacks. Yet the historian could argue that *Titus Andronicus*, like the late moralities or *Doctor Faustus*, is more "Elizabethan" than those mature tragedies because the dominant assumptions of the age have not yet been transformed or disguised by Shakespeare's art. The apparent accessibility of Hamlet's Denmark or Lear's England or Othello's Cyprus to our view only makes our unacknowledged spectacles more insidious.

Lest I be misunderstood, let me state emphatically that I am *not* arguing that our notions of character or plot or dramatic logic are irrelevant to the drama in the age of Shakespeare. Rather, I *am* arguing that our unexamined assumptions cannot fully account for Elizabethan characters or plots or dramatic logic. For example, we cannot flatly assume that every event in an Elizabethan play is part of a psychological progression, an unfolding of character as in a novel by Henry James. As noted in the previous chapter, minor figures (like Philario or Priam) or even major figures (like Cleopatra or Hector) can for a moment cease to be important as individuals but instead can participate in some larger, shared effect achieved by an entire scene or grouping (as also suggested by the Peacham drawing). If we are unwilling to transcend our terms, we may never be able to see the logic behind Feste's "unnecessary" disguise as Sir Topas or Antony's decision to fight at sea or Hector's capitulation to Paris and Troilus. Similarly, the modern reader can miss obvious, striking meanings in Prince Hal's manipulation of Francis or Gloucester's "fall" where our sense of character is superseded by some other principle we may not take into account. As with Martius and Quintus at the bloody pit, there may be a revealing logic or a carefully wrought pattern behind such distinctive moments, which may be obscured by the spectacles of realism.

To return one last time to Hamlet and the prayer scene, the director, even after recognizing the link, may still find an *exact* duplication in the staging of Hamlet/Claudius and Pyrrhus/Priam to be a disconcerting violation of realism and conventional stage practice. The actor, seeking his "feel" for the scene, is quite rightly concerned with the prince's state of mind and emotional rhythms and will not want to be constrained by the staging of an earlier moment. In various ways, to have identical staging and blocking in the two scenes cuts against the modern grain. I am not arguing that the concerns here of director and actor are unimportant. But the modern sense of character and flow and subtext should not screen out *everything* else, so that Hamlet obscures *Hamlet*. There *is* a larger pattern, of which this scene is an important part, and many significant meanings can be realized only if a production (or a critical essay) realizes both the insights sought by the modern reader *and* the patterned logic woven into the fabric by the original craftsman. Again, the open stage, once we truly learn to use it, can yield both kinds of meanings to the viewer's eye.

In conclusion, I can acknowledge the inevitability of distortion when we read the literature, and especially the drama, of the past. Automatically, we make adjustments when we pick up a copy of Homer or Dante or Shakespeare or Milton. We don our spectacles. But my final question is: how much distortion are we willing to allow? We can chuckle at the Victorians when they bowdlerize Shakespeare (for example, eliminating the word "whore" from *Othello*), but the modern critic or director or reader may be guilty of less obvious but equivalent sins against the text. To be conscious of the viewer's eye and the spectacles of realism is at least to transcend our two-dimensional attitude toward the words and our unwarranted sense of progress and superiority. In his dedicatory poem to the First Folio, Jonson described Shakespeare as "not of an age, but for all time." If Shakespeare and his contemporaries are to be understood fully and sympathetically in *our* time, the modern reader must master not only the poetry and allusions and characters and plots but also the larger theatrical language that can transcend the printed page and the distinctive logic that can transcend the limits of realism. Otherwise, we may unwittingly be acting out our own analogue—linking ourselves not to Pyrrhus or the horseboy but rather to those laughable readers of bygone days who could not break free from their own limited conceptions of drama and therefore could never fully comprehend the mirror Shakespeare held up to nature.

Bibliography

The list of books and essays that follows is highly selective. Given the large number of plays dealt with, often briefly, in my study, I have chosen not to list critical essays on individual plays (such as the many discussions of Gloucester at Dover Cliffs) unless some larger point is at stake. Also omitted are well-known standard works (like *The Elizabethan Stage*) and studies devoted primarily to stage history (the work of Arthur Colby Sprague or Marvin Rosenberg) or to the physical characteristics of the Elizabethan theaters. Rather, I have sought to isolate in my headings some major strands of my argument and have then emphasized, with a few notable exceptions, recent scholarship.

I. The Modern Stage Quarrel: The Critic, the Director, and the Historian

Annan, N. G. "The Marlowe Society Tradition." *Cambridge Journal* 3 (1950): 592–612.

Beckerman, Bernard. "The Flowers of Fancy, the Jerks of Invention, or, Directorial Approaches to Shakespeare." In *Shakespeare 1971*, edited by Clifford Leech and J. M. R. Margeson, pp. 200–214. Toronto and Buffalo: University of Toronto Press, 1972.

Bentley, Gerald Eades. "Shakespeare and the Readers of His Plays," *Shakespeare and His Theatre*, pp. 1–26. Lincoln: University of Nebraska Press, 1964.

Brook, Peter. *The Empty Space*. New York: Atheneum, 1968.

Brown, John Russell. *Free Shakespeare*. London: Heinemann, 1974.

———. "Theater Research and the Criticism of Shakespeare and His Contemporaries." *Shakespeare Quarterly* 13 (1962): 451–61.

———. "The Theatrical Element of Shakespeare Criticism." In *Reinterpretations of Elizabethan Drama*, edited by Norman Rabkin, pp. 177–95. Selected Papers from the English Institute. New York and London: Columbia University Press, 1969.

Byrne, M. St. Clare. "Dramatic Intention and Theatrical Realization." In *The Triple Bond*, edited by Joseph G. Price, pp. 30–49. University Park and London: Pennsylvania State University Press, 1975.

Carlisle, Carol Jones. *Shakespeare from the Greenroom: Actors' Criticisms of*

Four Major Tragedies. Chapel Hill: University of North Carolina Press, 1969.

Chinoy, Helen Krich. "The Director as Mythagog: Jonathan Miller Talks about Directing Shakespeare." *Shakespeare Quarterly* 27 (1976): 7–14.

Evans, Gareth Lloyd. "Interpretation or Experience? Shakespeare at Stratford." *Shakespeare Survey* 23 (1970): 131–35.

Hapgood, Robert. "Shakespeare and the Included Spectator." In *Reinterpretations of Elizabethan Drama*, edited by Norman Rabkin, pp. 117–36. Selected Papers from the English Institute. New York and London: Columbia University Press, 1969.

Harbage, Alfred. "The Role of the Shakespearean Producer." *Shakespeare Jahrbuch* 91 (1955): 161–73.

Hauger, George. "Theatre in General," *Theatre—General and Particular*, pp. 14–47. London: Michael Joseph, 1966.

Jones, Emrys. "The Scenic Poet," *Scenic Form in Shakespeare*, pp. 3–40. Oxford: Clarendon Press, 1971.

Lyons, Clifford. "Shakespeare's Plays: 'devis'd and play'd to take spectators'—Some Critical Implications." *Renaissance Papers 1968*, edited by George Walton Williams, pp. 55–63. The Southeastern Renaissance Conference, 1969.

Mack, Maynard. "Actors and Redactors," *"King Lear" in Our Time*, pp. 1–41. Berkeley and Los Angeles: University of California Press, 1965.

Marsh, Robert. "Historical Interpretation and the History of Criticism." In *Literary Criticism and Historical Understanding*, edited by Phillip Damon, pp. 1–24. Selected Papers from the English Institute. New York and London: Columbia University Press, 1967.

Muir, Kenneth. "The Critic, the Director, and Liberty of Interpreting." In *The Triple Bond*, edited by Joseph Price, pp. 20–29. University Park and London: Pennsylvania State University Press, 1975.

Price, Joseph G. "The Interpretation of Shakespeare in the Theatre." In *Directions in Literary Criticism*, edited by Stanley Weintraub and Philip Young, pp. 70–84. University Park and London: Pennsylvania State University Press, 1973.

Prior, Moody E. "Page vs. Stage: The Province of the Critic of Shakespeare." *University of Denver Quarterly* 10 (1975): 75–81.

Rabkin, Norman. "Meaning and Shakespeare." In *Shakespeare 1971*, edited by Clifford Leech and J. M. R. Margeson, pp. 89–106. Toronto and Buffalo: University of Toronto Press, 1972.

Robertson, D. W., Jr. "Some Observations on Method in Literary Studies." *New Literary History* 1 (1969): 21–33.

Seltzer, Daniel. "Shakespeare's Texts and Modern Productions." In *Reinterpretations of Elizabethan Drama*, edited by Norman Rabkin, pp. 89–115. Selected Papers from the English Institute. New York and London: Columbia University Press, 1969.

Thomson, Peter. "Shakespeare Straight and Crooked: A Review of the 1973 Season at Stratford." *Shakespeare Survey* 27 (1974): 143–46.

Wells, Stanley. "The Academic and the Theatre." In *The Triple Bond*, edited by Joseph G. Price, pp. 3–19. University Park and London: Pennsylvania State University Press, 1975.

_____. *Literature and Drama*. London: Routledge & Kegan Paul, 1970.

Weimann, Robert. "Past Significance and Present Meaning in Literary History." *New Literary History* 1 (1969): 91–109.

_____. "Shakespeare on the Modern Stage: Past Significance and Present Meaning." *Shakespeare Survey* 20 (1967): 113–20.

II. The Contribution of the Popular Dramatic Tradition

Bethell, S. L. *Shakespeare and the Popular Dramatic Tradition*. London and New York: Staples Press, 1944.

Bevington, David M. *From "Mankind" to Marlowe: Growth of Structure in the Popular Drama of Tudor England*. Cambridge, Mass.: Harvard University Press, 1962.

Craik, T. W. *The Tudor Interlude: Stage, Costume, and Acting*. Leicester University Press, 1962.

Dessen, Alan C. "The Dramatic Legacy of the Elizabethan Morality," *Jonson's Moral Comedy*, pp. 8–36. Evanston: Northwestern University Press, 1971.

_____. "The Morall as an Elizabethan Dramatic Kind: An Exploratory Essay." *Comparative Drama* 5 (1971): 138–59.

Habicht, Werner. "The *Wit*-Interludes and the Form of Pre-Shakespearean 'Romantic Comedy'." *Renaissance Drama* 8 (1965): 73–88.

Jones, Robert C. "Dangerous Sport: The Audience's Engagement with Vice in the Moral Interludes." *Renaissance Drama* N.S. 6 (1973): 45–64.

Rossiter, A. P. *English Drama From Early Times to the Elizabethans*. London: Hutchinson & Co., 1950.

Spivack, Bernard. *Shakespeare and the Allegory of Evil: The History of a Metaphor in Relation to His Major Villains*. New York: Columbia University Press, 1958.

Talbert, Ernest William. *Elizabethan Drama and Shakespeare's Early Plays*. Chapel Hill: University of North Carolina Press, 1963.

Wickham, Glynne. *Shakespeare's Dramatic Heritage: Collected Studies in Mediaeval, Tudor and Shakespearean Drama*. New York: Barnes & Noble, 1969.

Wilson, F. P. *The English Drama 1485–1585*. New York and Oxford: Oxford University Press, 1969.

III. *Staging and Stagecraft in Elizabethan Drama*

Armstrong, William A. "Actors and Theatres." *Shakespeare Survey* 17 (1964): 191–204.

———. "Ben Jonson and Jacobean Stagecraft." In *Jacobean Theatre*, edited by John Russell Brown and Bernard Harris, pp. 43–61. New York: Capricorn Books, 1967.

Beckerman, Bernard. *Shakespeare at the Globe 1599–1609*. New York: Macmillan, 1962.

Bradbrook, Muriel C. *Elizabethan Stage Conditions*. Cambridge: Cambridge University Press, 1932.

———. *Themes and Conventions of Elizabethan Tragedy*. Cambridge: Cambridge University Press, 1935.

Brown, John Russell. *Shakespeare's Dramatic Style*. New York: Barnes & Noble, 1972.

———. *Shakespeare's Plays in Performance*. London: Edward Arnold, 1966.

Coghill, Nevill. *Shakespeare's Professional Skills*. Cambridge: Cambridge University Press, 1964.

Granville-Barker, Harley. "A Note Upon Chapters XX. and XXI. of *The Elizabethan Stage*." *Review of English Studies* 1 (1925): 60–71.

———. *Prefaces to Shakespeare*. 2 vols. Princeton: Princeton University Press, 1946.

Greenfield, Thelma N. *The Induction in Elizabethan Drama*. Eugene: University of Oregon Books, 1969.

Griffin, Alice Venezky. *Pageantry on the Shakespearean Stage*. New York: Twayne, 1951.

Gurr, Andrew. *The Shakespearean Stage 1574–1642*. Cambridge: Cambridge University Press, 1970.

Habicht, Werner. "Tree Properties and Tree Scenes in Elizabethan Theater." *Renaissance Drama* N.S. 4 (1971): 69–92.

Harbage, Alfred. *Theatre for Shakespeare*. Toronto: University of Toronto Press, 1955.

Hosley, Richard. "The Playhouses and the Stage." In *A New Companion to Shakespeare Studies*, edited by Kenneth Muir and S. Schoenbaum, pp. 15–34. Cambridge: Cambridge University Press, 1971.

Joseph, Bertram. "The Elizabethan Stage and Acting." In *The Age of Shakespeare*, edited by Boris Ford, pp. 147–61. Pelican Guide to English Literature. Baltimore: Penguin, 1960.

Kernodle, George R. "The Open Stage: Elizabethan or Existentialist?" *Shakespeare Survey* 12 (1959): 1–7.

King, T. J. *Shakespearean Staging, 1599–1642.* Cambridge, Mass.: Harvard University Press, 1971.

_____. "The Stage in the Time of Shakespeare: A Survey of Major Scholarship." *Renaissance Drama* N.S. 4 (1971): 199–235.

Knight, G. Wilson. *Shakespearian Production with Especial Reference to the Tragedies.* London: Faber & Faber, 1964.

Kolin, Philip C.; and Wyatt, R. O., II. "A Bibliography of Scholarship on the Elizabethan Stage Since Chambers." *Research Opportunities in Renaissance Drama* 15–16 (1972–73): 33–59.

Lawrence, William J. *Pre-Restoration Stage Studies.* Cambridge, Mass.: Harvard University Press, 1927.

Linthicum, M. Channing. *Costume in the Drama of Shakespeare and His Contemporaries.* Oxford: Clarendon Press, 1936.

Mehl, Dieter. *The Elizabethan Dumb Show.* London: Methuen, 1965.

Mitchell, Lee. "Shakespeare's Lighting Effects." *Speech Monographs* 15 (1948): 72–84.

Nicoll, Allardyce. "'Passing Over the Stage'." *Shakespeare Survey* 12 (1959): 47–55.

Reynolds, George Fullmer. *On Shakespeare's Stage.* Boulder: University of Colorado Press, 1967.

_____. *The Staging of Elizabethan Plays at the Red Bull Theater 1605–1625.* New York: Modern Language Association of America, 1940.

Ross, Lawrence J. "The Use of a 'Fit-Up' Booth in *Othello*." *Shakespeare Quarterly* 12 (1961): 359–70.

Rothwell, W. F. "Was There a Typical Elizabethan Stage?" *Shakespeare Survey* 12 (1959): 15–21.

Saunders, J. W. "Staging at the Globe, 1599–1613." *Shakespeare Quarterly* 11 (1960): 401–25.

_____. "Vaulting the Rails." *Shakespeare Survey* 7 (1954): 69–81.

Seltzer, Daniel. "The Actors and Staging." In *A New Companion to Shakespeare Studies*, edited by Kenneth Muir and S. Schoenbaum, pp. 35–54. Cambridge: Cambridge University Press, 1971.

Simmons, J. L. "Elizabethan Stage Practice and Marlowe's *The Jew of Malta*." *Renaissance Drama* N.S. 4 (1971): 93–104.

Smith, Hal H. "Some Principles of Elizabethan Stage Costume." *Journal of the Warburg and Courtauld Institutes* 25 (1962): 240–57.

Smith, Warren D. *Shakespeare's Playhouse Practice: A Handbook*. Hanover, N.H.: University Press of New England, 1975.

Southern, Richard. *The Staging of Plays before Shakespeare*. London: Faber & Faber, 1973.

Stamm, Rudolf. "Elizabethan Stage-Practice and the Transmutation of Source Material by the Dramatists." *Shakespeare Survey* 12 (1959): 64–70.

Styan, J. L. *Drama, Stage and Audience*. London and New York: Cambridge University Press, 1975.

————. *Shakespeare's Stagecraft*. Cambridge: Cambridge University Press, 1967.

Watkins, Ronald. *On Producing Shakespeare*. London: Michael Joseph, 1950.

————; and Lemmon, Jeremy. *The Poet's Method*. Totowa, N.J.: Rowman & Littlefield, 1974.

Wickham, Glynne. *Early English Stages 1300–1660: Volume Two 1576 to 1660*. Parts I and II. New York: Columbia University Press, 1963, 1972.

IV. Analogous Action and Multiple Unity

Aldus, Paul J. "Analogical Probability in Shakespeare's Plays." *Shakespeare Quarterly* 6 (1955): 397–414.

Black, James. "The Visual Artistry of *Romeo and Juliet*." *Studies in English Literature* 15 (1975): 245–56.

Doran, Madeleine. *Endeavors of Art: A Study of Form in Elizabethan Drama*. Madison: University of Wisconsin Press, 1954.

Empson, William. "Double Plots: Heroic and Pastoral in the Main Plot and Sub-Plot," *Some Versions of Pastoral*, pp. 25–86. London: Chatto & Windus, 1935.

Levin, Lawrence L. "Replication as Dramatic Strategy in the Comedies of Ben Jonson." *Renaissance Drama* N.S. 5 (1972): 37–74.

Levin, Richard. *The Multiple Plot in English Renaissance Drama*. Chicago and London: University of Chicago Press, 1971.

Mack, Maynard. "The Jacobean Shakespeare: Some observations on the construction of the Tragedies." In *Jacobean Theatre*, edited by John Russell Brown and Bernard Harris, pp. 11–41. New York: Capricorn Books, 1967.

Pearce, Frances M. "Analogical Probability and the Clown in *All's Well That Ends Well*." *Shakespeare Jahrbuch* 108 (1972): 129–44.

Price, Hereward T. "Mirror-Scenes in Shakespeare." In *Joseph Quincy*

Adams Memorial Studies, edited by James G. McManaway, Giles E. Dawson, and Edwin E. Willoughby, pp. 101–13. Washington, D.C.: The Folger Shakespeare Library, 1948.

Rabkin, Norman. "The Double Plot: Notes on the History of a Convention." *Renaissance Drama* 7 (1964): 55–69.

Rose, Mark. *Shakespearean Design*. Cambridge, Mass.: Harvard University Press, 1972.

Shaw, John. "The Staging of Parody and Parallels in 'I Henry IV'." *Shakespeare Survey* 20 (1967): 61–73.

V. Imagery for the Viewer's Eye

Charney, Maurice. *Shakespeare's Roman Plays: The Function of Imagery in the Drama*. Cambridge, Mass.: Harvard University Press, 1961.

———. *Style in "Hamlet."* Princeton: Princeton University Press, 1969.

Dessen, Alan C. "Hamlet's Poisoned Sword: A Study in Dramatic Imagery." *Shakespeare Studies* 5 (1969): 53–69.

———. "Two Falls and a Trap: Shakespeare and the Spectacles of Realism." *English Literary Renaissance* 5 (1975): 291–307.

Doebler, John. *Shakespeare's Speaking Pictures: Studies in Iconic Imagery*. Albuquerque: University of New Mexico Press, 1974.

Downer, Alan S. "The Life of Our Design: The Function of Imagery in the Poetic Drama." *Hudson Review* 2 (1949): 242–63.

Ewbank, Inga-Stina. "'More Pregnantly Than Words': Some Uses and Limitations of Visual Symbolism." *Shakespeare Survey* 24 (1971): 13–18.

Fleischer, Martha Hester. *The Iconography of the English History Play*. Salzburg Studies in English Literature. Salzburg, 1974.

———. "Stage Imagery." In *The Reader's Encyclopedia of Shakespeare*, edited by Oscar James Campbell and Edward G. Quinn, pp. 819–20. New York: Thomas Y. Crowell, 1966.

Foakes, R. A. "Suggestions for a New Approach to Shakespeare's Imagery." *Shakespeare Survey* 5 (1952): 81–92.

Lyons, Clifford. "Stage Imagery in Shakespeare's Plays." In *Essays on Shakespeare and Elizabethan Drama in Honor of Hardin Craig*, edited by Richard Hosley, pp. 261–74. Columbia, Mo.: University of Missouri Press, 1962.

Mehl, Dieter. "Emblems in English Renaissance Drama." *Renaissance Drama* N.S. 2 (1969): 39–57.

———. "Visual and Rhetorical Imagery in Shakespeare's Plays." *Essays and Studies* 25 (1972): 83–100.

Merchant, W. Moelwyn. *Shakespeare and the Artist*. London: Oxford University Press, 1959.

Powell, Jocelyn. "Marlowe's Spectacle." *Tulane Drama Review* 8 (1964): 195–210.

Reibetanz, John. "Theatrical Emblems in *King Lear*." In *Some Facets of "King Lear": Essays in Prismatic Criticism*, edited by Rosalie L. Colie and F. T. Flahiff, pp. 39–57. Toronto: University of Toronto Press, 1974.

Salomon, Brownell. "Visual and Aural Signs in the Performed English Renaissance Play." *Renaissance Drama* N.S. 5 (1972): 143–69.

Index

173